Hiking the Four Corners

Apr 2015

Hiking
the Four Corners

A Guide to the Area's
Greatest Hiking Adventures

JD Tanner and Emily Ressler-Tanner

FALCONGUIDES

GUILFORD, CONNECTICUT
HELENA, MONTANA

An imprint of Rowman & Littlefield
Falcon, FalconGuides, and Outfit Your Mind are registered trademarks of Rowman & Littlefield.

Distributed by NATIONAL BOOK NETWORK

Copyright © 2015 by Rowman & Littlefield
Photos by JD Tanner and Emily Ressler-Tanner
Maps by Alena Joy Pearce © Rowman & Littlefield

British Library Cataloguing-in-Publication Information available

Library of Congress Cataloging-in-Publication Data available
ISBN 978-0-7627-9194-1 (paperback)

∞™ The paper used in this publication meets the minimum requirements of American National Standard for Information Sciences—Permanence of Paper for Printed Library Materials, ANSI/NISO Z39.48-1992.

Contents

The Hikes

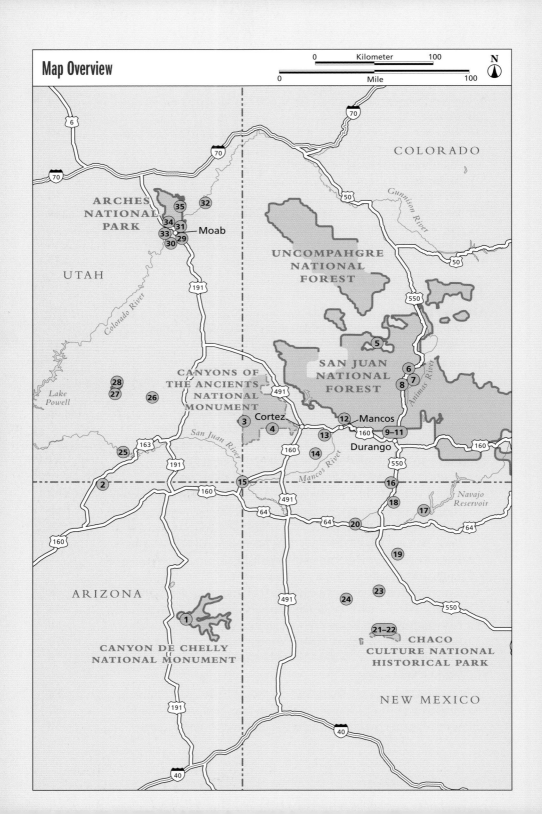

Acknowledgments

We would like to send out a special thank-you to all the land managers who patiently answered our questions, pointed us toward the very best trails, and carefully reviewed the trail descriptions for this guide. We would also like to thank our friends and family for accompanying us on many of the trails in the Four Corners; your company, humor, support, and enthusiasm were very much appreciated. Finally, we would like to thank all of our friends at FalconGuides, particularly David Legere, Katie Benoit, Max Phelps, and Julie Marsh, for their support and encouragement and for making a book out of our rough manuscript.

◄ *Erosion-carved rock formation (hike 24)*

Introduction

The Four Corners region is a vast physiographic and geologic highland region located in the southwestern United States. The region includes much of southeastern Utah, southwestern Colorado, northwestern New Mexico, and northeastern Arizona. The boundaries of these four states intersect in a remote area of the Navajo Nation. The Four Corners gets its name from this quadripoint, which forms four right angles and is unique in that it is the only place in the United States where you can be in four states at the same time. The Four Corners Monument, one of several parks managed by Navajo Parks and Recreation, marks this distinctive landmark.

The area known collectively as the Four Corners region is part of the larger geographic area known as the Colorado Plateau. The Colorado Plateau covers over 130,000 square miles and is home to more National Park Service (NPS) units than any other region of the United States. Many of these NPS units are located in the Four Corners region and are highlighted in this guide, including Arches National Park, Mesa Verde National Park, Hovenweep National Monument, Natural Bridges National Monument, Canyons of the Ancients National Monument, Chaco Culture National Historical Park, Aztec Ruins National Monument, Canyon de Chelly National Monument, and Navajo National Monument.

The region is home to many tribal lands and nations, including the Navajo, Jicarilla Apache, Hopi, Southern Ute, Mountain Ute, and Zuni. The largest of these entities is the Navajo Nation, which covers more than 27,000 square miles of land in the states of Arizona, Utah, and New Mexico.

We couldn't be more excited to introduce you to the extensive network of trails offered here in the Four Corners region. Hiking opportunities are virtually unlimited in this region, and the landscape offers endless beauty and solitude for outdoor enthusiasts. Trails here follow towering sandstone cliffs, traverse quiet valleys and cool canyons, and climb over rough and rugged mountain terrain to some of the most spectacular scenery in the world. Those willing to venture to this hard-to-reach region will be rewarded with a multitude of recreational opportunities. Springs, arches, natural bridges, narrow canyons, ancient ruins, clear-flowing streams, and geologic wonders are the natural gems of the Four Corners and are all highlighted in this guide.

If you are a visitor to the Four Corners, this collection of hiking trails will serve as a valuable tool for familiarizing yourself with the great variety of outdoor adventures within this vast region. Our hope is that this guide will serve as your introduction to the region's adventures and will keep you returning to the Four Corners region time and time again. If you are a longtime local of the area, we hope this book will take you on some new adventures to some lesser-known trails in this diverse region.

◀ *Petroglyph Point Trail (hike 14)*

This guide lists easy, moderate, and more challenging hikes in the Four Corners region. Some of the hikes can be found near the more populated towns of the region, including Moab, Utah; Durango, Colorado; and Farmington, New Mexico. Some trails are near the most popular vacation destinations, such as Mesa Verde and Arches National Parks, while others are located in more remote and seldom-visited areas and will likely require a good bit of driving to reach the trailhead. All showcase the natural wonders hidden in this region. From majestic mountain peaks to hidden sandstone canyons, the hikes featured in the pages of this book are some of the best hikes in the region. No matter where you choose to explore, you will be rewarded with brilliant memories and leave with a desire to return. Ask almost any outdoor enthusiast who has spent time here, and they will tell you that this rugged landscape has a way of getting a hold on your heart and soul.

We have done our best to include a little something for everyone and have tried to select trails from many parts of the region while still making sure to include those trails widely considered to be superior for their scenic and historical significance. Hikes for families, for nature lovers, for scenic views, and for history buffs have all been included and should be considered an introduction to the area and a starting point to continue your explorations in the Four Corners.

May your trails be crooked, winding, lonesome, dangerous, leading to the most amazing view. May your mountains rise into and above the clouds.
—Edward Abbey

This famous quote by American author and environmentalist Edward Abbey is the perfect way to start this guide. After all, Abbey used these words in his book *Desert Solitaire: A Season in the Wilderness*, which details Abbey's time in parts of the region, most notably Arches National Park. It is truly our wish to you that you find the areas in this guide as wonderful and wild as we have.

Weather

Hikers come to the Four Corners region year-round, but most come during spring, summer, and autumn. Since the region is a high desert environment, with daytime high temperatures often reaching 95°F to 105°F almost daily from June through August, summer is the most unfavorable time of the year to hike in the area. The exception is hikes at higher elevation ranges, where summer temperatures can be very mild.

Spring and autumn are the best hiking seasons for desert trips in the Four Corners region. Spring weather (March through May) can be highly variable, with daytime high temperatures ranging from the 50s to the 70s and nighttime lows ranging from 20° to 50°. Occasional cold fronts from the west and northwest can bring cold, windy conditions; rain showers at the lower elevations; and perhaps snow on the higher mesas, particularly in March and April. Snow will be present through early summer for all mountain hikes. Generally, warm, dry weather prevails between storm systems.

Early spring is one of the best times of the year to hike in the canyons of the region. Springs and seasonal streams are likely to be flowing, and slickrock water pockets will hold rainwater longer at this time of year, providing more flexibility and a margin of safety in the backcountry.

The onset of searing summer heat at lower elevations usually begins in late May, and it can persist into mid-September. Hikes at higher elevations may be quite pleasant. The monsoon season usually begins in mid-July and ends in mid-September. Moist tropical air masses over Mexico circulate an almost daily parade of thunderstorms over the region. Midsummer weather in the region can be characterized by heavy rainfall, which is usually accompanied by strong, gusty winds and lightning.

Autumn provides some of the most stable weather of the year. Clear, warm, sunny days and cool nights make this one of the most delightful seasons to visit the Four Corners region. Expect daytime highs to range from the 70s and 80s in September to the 40s and 50s by November. Overnight lows are typically in the 20° to 50° range. Only the most active summer monsoon season will help recharge springs and streams, but the deepest water pockets often persist into early fall due to cooler temperatures and reduced evaporation. Cold fronts can sweep through the region as autumn progresses, and by mid- to late October in some years, these fronts can drop temperatures significantly for several days or longer. Snowfall in the higher elevations above 5,000 to 6,000 feet is not uncommon.

Winter in the Four Corners region is cold and often windy, and deep snow sometimes covers the ground above 6,000 feet. To stay up to date on weather conditions, listen to local radio stations while driving and check with Bureau of Land Management (BLM) and NPS offices for current forecasts. The National Oceanic and Atmospheric Administration is a good resource for current weather forecasts in the area (www.noaa.gov).

Weather Averages for Page, Arizona

Month	High	Low	Rainfall (in.)
January	45	27	0.69
February	51	31	0.55
March	61	38	0.56
April	70	45	0.55
May	81	55	0.41
June	92	64	0.11
July	96	70	0.57
August	93	68	0.86
September	85	60	0.70
October	70	48	1.01
November	55	36	0.46
December	44	28	0.38

(Statistics from the Weather Channel, March 2014)

Weather Averages for Durango, Colorado

Month	High	Low	Rainfall (in.)
January	40	12	1.65
February	47	17	1.50
March	54	24	1.71
April	63	30	1.30
May	71	36	1.17
June	81	43	0.61
July	85	51	1.64
August	83	50	2.58
September	76	42	1.94
October	66	31	2.10
November	51	21	1.82
December	41	13	1.37

(Statistics from the Weather Channel, March 2014)

Weather Averages for Farmington, New Mexico

Month	High	Low	Rainfall (in.)
January	41	20	0.53
February	47	25	0.61
March	56	30	0.78
April	65	36	0.65
May	75	46	0.54
June	85	55	0.21
July	90	61	0.90
August	87	60	1.26
September	79	52	1.04
October	66	40	0.91
November	52	29	0.68
December	41	21	0.50

(Statistics from the Weather Channel, March 2014)

Weather Averages for Moab, Utah

Month	High	Low	Rainfall (in.)
January	43	20	0.63
February	52	26	0.66
March	63	35	0.83
April	72	42	0.83
May	83	50	0.70
June	93	58	0.41
July	99	64	0.97
August	96	63	0.97
September	87	53	0.86
October	73	41	1.17
November	56	30	0.76
December	44	21	0.69

(Statistics from the Weather Channel, March 2014)

Horny toad

Flora and Fauna

The flora of the Four Corners region reflects the diversity of environmental conditions here. Elevations vary greatly in this region, and plant communities range from cool forests to desert shrublands.

The high elevations support well-developed conifer forests in the transition zone. Ponderosa pine dominates this transition zone, and in the most sheltered locations, Douglas fir and the occasional white fir join the forest. In the microclimates that mimic much higher elevations, such as cool, sheltered draws, Engelmann spruce and blue spruce appear. These conifer forests reach well into the canyons, lending to their sandstone gorges an atmosphere of cool mountains. Quaking aspen are common in this zone, displaying golden foliage in early autumn.

Spring in the desert

Prickly pear cactus in bloom

Wildlife in this zone is typical of any high mountain region in the West. Black bears, elk, mule deer, and mountain lions are common, and these large mammals may extend their range into neighboring canyons. Reptiles are almost absent in this zone, save for the short-horned lizard and the Great Basin rattlesnake, a rare sight in these forests.

Most of the region lies within the Upper Sonoran zone, and its pinyon-juniper woodlands are more widespread in the Southwestern and Intermountain Regions than any other forest type. It extends from about 4,500 feet to 7,000 feet in elevation and is characterized by the two-needled Colorado pinyon and the Utah juniper. Due to the trees' small, uniform size (they rarely exceed 20 feet in height), the woodland has been dubbed the "pygmy forest."

The open brushlands of the cool desert shrub and sand desert shrub communities occupy the lower-elevation mesas, canyons, and terraces, generally below 4,500 feet, but often mixing with the pinyon-juniper woodland at higher elevations. The cool desert shrub community is dominated by big sagebrush in its upper elevations and by black brush in the warmer, drier, and lower elevations. Four-wing saltbush occupies sites where saline soils dominate. Mormon tea, yucca, and various cacti cover the landscape. Between the coarse, widely scattered shrubs in this community is a variety of native bunchgrasses.

Most desert plants are succulents and have fleshy leaves or stems that allow them to store water in their tissues. Cacti are the most obvious example. They have shallow but wide spreading root systems that allow them to absorb moisture from even the lightest rainfall.

The Lower Sonoran zone occurs in the lowest elevations in the region and is limited to areas surrounding Lake Powell and Lees Ferry. This is the hottest and driest part of Glen Canyon, and it is a true desert environment. Dominant plants include shadscale, blackbrush, Mormon tea, and yucca. Rabbitbrush and arrow weed are common in open canyon bottoms, particularly along the Paria River near Lees Ferry.

A variety of lizards are frequent trail companions in this zone. Gopher snakes and striped whipsnakes inhabit dry areas, while garter snakes prefer riparian environments. Great Basin and western rattlesnakes inhabit the western reaches of the region, while the midget faded rattlesnake is most common in southeastern Utah. Amphibians are common in riparian habitats, and you will see the tadpoles and adults of the red-spotted and Great Basin spadefoot toads, western leopard frog, and canyon tree frog.

Large mammals include mule deer, which range well into many canyons and are sometimes followed by a mountain lion. Smaller mammals include the black-tailed jackrabbit, rock squirrel, deer mouse, desert wood rat, antelope ground squirrel, chipmunk, coyote, and beaver in the lower canyons, particularly near Lake Powell.

Wilderness Restrictions/Regulations

The hiking trails in this book traverse through lands that are controlled and managed by various public agencies. Each group has its own rules and regulations that must be respected and adhered to at all times while hiking on these lands. The trails in this book cross through lands managed by the United States Forest Service, the National Park Service, state park systems, the Bureau of Land Management, and a couple of city park systems. Hikes on lands managed by the NPS will have firmer rules and regulations in regards to recreation and land-use restrictions.

When day hiking, you generally do not need permits to enjoy many of the trails in this book, although many land managers do request that you register at the trailhead. If you plan to embark on a long-distance hiking trip, you will want to call the managing office of the area that you are hiking through and secure a backcountry permit for the area. You may be required to reserve your campsites for each night that you will be camping along the trail. The USDA Forest Service lands are typically less strict about camping and usually allow dispersed, primitive camping along the trails as long as you are not within a particular distance from waterways, the trail, roads, and other specified areas. Before embarking on a hiking trip, plan ahead by checking the website or calling the office of the management agency of the lands you will be traversing. They will provide the most up-to-date information on regulations and trail conditions.

Be sure to sign in at all trailhead registers.

Hazards

While several of the hikes in this book are just minutes from civilization, most are in remote areas that may present hazardous conditions. Unexpected injury or illness, extreme heat, heavy rains or snow, flash floods, lack of water, dehydration, and encounters with poisonous creatures or spiny cacti can all stop you in your tracks.

Always obtain up-to-date information on trails, routes, road conditions, and water availability from the land management agencies listed in this guide. Since conditions are constantly changing, this book is no substitute for updated information. Before you leave home, let a family member, friend, or employer know where you are going and when you plan to return. Make arrangements so that if you do not return home or contact that person by a certain time, he or she will initiate search-and-rescue operations. Upon returning from your trip, be sure to notify that person to avoid an unnecessary search. Always sign trailhead registers where available. Information from trailhead registers has helped to locate and save many overdue hikers.

Flash floods are always a danger to be reckoned with, and as little as 0.25 to 0.5 inch of rain falling in a short period of time can result in a newborn stream coursing down a dry wash. Be aware of dry washes (or arroyos) even if it is not raining where you are, since rain in a different location can funnel large amounts of water downstream. A moderate rain lasting 2 to 3 hours can result in a significant flash flood. During the summer monsoon season (generally from mid-July through mid-September), torrents of rain are unleashed from towering thunderheads in hit-and-miss fashion throughout the region.

Lightning often occurs with summer thunderstorms. Keep your eye on the sky: Dark cumulonimbus clouds herald the approach of a thunderstorm. If one is approaching, stay away from ridges, mesa tops, the bases of cliffs, solitary trees, shallow overhangs and alcoves, and open areas. Seek shelter in thickets of brush or in pinyon-juniper woodlands where the trees are plentiful, small, and of uniform size. In the absence of that kind of shelter, retreat to a boulder field or low-lying area. Keep in mind that, contrary to myth, lightning often strikes repeatedly in the same location.

The Four Corners region also has its share of cacti, thorny shrubs, and biting insects that can injure you if you are careless. Biting flies and gnats are common throughout the region. Deer flies and sand flies are aggressive, carnivorous, and common in sandy areas of washes during the warmest months of the year, generally from June through mid-September. The best defense is a long-sleeved shirt and lightweight long pants. During warmer months you may encounter mosquitoes, usually only in limited numbers, primarily near water sources.

Various spiders (including the black widow and tarantula), scorpions, and centipedes inhabit the region. Scorpions are the most common. Most can inflict a painful sting, but their venom is rarely life-threatening. Scorpions spend the day in the shade in dark crevices under rocks, logs, and bark. Be careful where you put your hands and feet, and avoid picking up rocks. Be careful at night, and look before you sit. In the morning it is a good idea to check your shoes or boots for these critters before sticking your feet in them.

Ants are also prevalent throughout the area. Red harvester ants can inflict a memorable sting, and tiny red ants may march toward your pack and food.

Several species of poisonous snakes are found in the region, but pose a minimal threat to hikers. Your best bet is to avoid stepping on a snake and to leave them alone when you do see them. Most snakebites are the result of people trying to pick them up. Snakes rest in the shade to avoid midday heat, so use caution when stepping over logs and boulders and watch where you put your hands and feet.

Beware of the spines of cacti and yucca. Although cactus spines are painful, they can usually be removed with tweezers. The glochids—those tiny hairlike spines—are more difficult to remove and cause painful irritation. Use adhesive tape to remove them, since probing with fingernails or tweezers often imbeds them deeper into your skin.

Yucca plants have large, stiff spines that can inflict a painful puncture wound. If one of these spines breaks off in any part of your body, it can be very difficult to remove and you may have to endure the discomfort until a doctor can remove it.

One of several different types of cacti found in the Four Corners

Poison ivy can be found along a handful of trails in this guide, and it is estimated that somewhere between 50 and 70 percent of people experience a physical reaction after coming in contact with the plant. Poison ivy can grow as a woody shrub up to 6 feet high or as a vine that clings to other trees and shrubs. While the old expression "Leaves of three, let it be" is good advice to follow, several other three-leafed plants grow in the region, so be sure to educate yourself about poison ivy before hitting the trail. If you are particularly sensitive to the plant, it is a good idea to keep a bottle of poison ivy soap in your vehicle and wash all exposed skin upon completion of your hike. Be sure to launder all hiking clothes separately from other clothes and in hot water to remove the poison ivy oils.

Hikers may encounter mountain lions and/or black bears on trails at higher elevations. Running into these animals is rare, and attacks are even rarer. Trails that traverse mountain lion and black bear habitat are generally labeled. The recommendations for hiking in black bear and mountain lion habitats are very similar: Avoid hiking alone, keep small children and pets close to you, and be aware of your surroundings. Never approach these animals; if the animal moves toward you, make yourself appear "bigger"; and fight back if you are attacked. For more information on hiking in mountain lion and black bear habitats, contact local land management agencies.

Other hazards you may encounter include (but are not limited to) steep drop-offs, severe snowstorms, and heat-related illnesses. As mentioned earlier, many of the hikes in this guide are in rural areas. Having a full tank of gas and being aware of the nearest medical facility are highly recommended.

Be Prepared

"Be prepared." The Boy Scouts say it, Leave No Trace says it, and the best outdoors people say it. Being prepared won't completely keep you out of harm's way when you're outdoors, but it will minimize the chances of finding yourself there. That being said, here are some things to consider:

- Speak with local land managers to get the most up-to-date information on road and trail conditions.

- Familiarize yourself with the basics of first aid (bites, stings, sprains, and breaks), carry a first aid kit, and know how to use it.

- Hydrate! No matter where or when you are hiking, you should always be carrying water with you. A standard is two liters per person per day.

- Be prepared to treat water on longer hikes. Rivers and streams in the Four Corners area are not safe to drink directly from. Iodine tablets are small, light, and easy to carry.

- Carry a backpack in order to store the Ten Essentials: map, compass, sunglasses/sunscreen, extra food and water, extra clothes, headlamp/flashlight, first aid kit, fire starter, matches, and knife.

Don't forget to pack a warm jacket, your cell phone, a trash bag, and a snack.

- Pack your cell phone (on vibrate) as a safety backup.
- Keep an eye on the kids. Having them carry a whistle, just in case, isn't the worst idea.
- Bring a leash, doggie bags, and extra water for your pets.

Zero Impact

This hiking guide will take you to historical sites, conservation areas, national natural landmarks, and many other places of natural and cultural significance. For that reason the importance of Zero Impact cannot be stressed enough. You are encouraged to carefully plan your trip so that you know as much as you possibly can about the area you will be visiting. Being aware of information such as the weather forecast, trail conditions, and water availability is an important factor in planning a successful trip.

Once you begin your hike, do your best to stick to trails so you do not inadvertently trample sensitive vegetation. Be prepared to pack out any trash that you bring with you, and remember, it never hurts to carry out trash that others may have left behind. Be extra careful when visiting sites of historical and natural importance. Leave everything as you found it, and never remove artifacts found in these sensitive areas.

Consider your impact on wildlife as you visit their homes, and be sure not to feed them, as this act is unhealthy for wildlife and dangerous for people. Respect other visitors and users as well by keeping your pets on a leash, stepping to the side of the trail to allow others to pass, and keeping noise to a minimum.

For more information on enjoying the outdoors responsibly, please visit the Leave No Trace Center for Outdoor Ethics website at https://lnt.org.

How to Use This Guide

Each region begins with a section introduction, where you're given a sweeping look at the lay of the land. After this general overview, specific hikes within that region are described. You'll learn about the terrain and what surprises each route has to offer.

This guide is designed to be simple and easy to use. Each hike is described with a map and summary information that delivers the trail's vital statistics including length, difficulty, fees and permits, park hours, canine compatibility, and trail contacts. Directions to the trailhead are also provided, along with a general description of what you'll see along the way. A detailed route finder (Miles and Directions) sets forth mileages between significant landmarks along the trail.

How the Hikes Were Chosen

This guide describes trails that are accessible to almost every hiker, whether visiting from out of town or a local resident. The hikes in this guide range in length from just over 1 mile to over 12 miles, and most are in the 3- to 6-mile range. Hikes range in difficulty from flat excursions perfect for a family outing to more challenging treks in the Rocky Mountains. While these trails are among the best, keep in mind that nearby trails, sometimes in the same park or sometimes in a neighboring open space, may offer options better suited to your needs. We've tried to include other great hikes in the Honorable Mention sections of the guide.

Selecting a Hike

Some would argue that no hike involving any kind of climbing is easy, but climbs are a fact of life in the Four Corners region. Trail difficulty is a highly subjective matter, but we've tried to give you an idea of what to expect on each hike. Below is a description of how trail difficulty is categorized for this guide.

Easy hikes are generally short and flat, taking no longer than an hour to complete.

Moderate hikes involve increased distance and relatively mild changes in elevation and will take 1 to 2 hours to complete.

More challenging hikes feature some steep stretches, greater distances, and generally take longer than 2 hours to complete.

Keep in mind that what you think is easy is entirely dependent on your level of fitness and the adequacy of your gear (primarily shoes). Use the trail's length as a gauge of its relative difficulty—even if climbing is involved, it won't be too strenuous if the hike is less than 1 mile long. Some of the longer hikes are more strenuous than others due to length and elevation changes. If you are hiking with a group, select a hike that's appropriate for the least fit and prepared in your party.

Approximate hiking times are based on the assumption that on flat ground, most walkers average 2 miles per hour. Adjust that rate by the steepness of the terrain and your level of fitness (subtract time if you're an aerobic animal and add time if you're hiking with kids), and you have a ballpark hiking duration. Be sure to add more time if you plan to picnic or take part in other activities like bird-watching, swimming, wandering, or photography.

Trail Finder

Best Hikes for Lakes, Rivers, and Waterfalls

Best Hikes for Ruins

Best Hikes for Children

Best Hikes for Great Views

Best Hikes for History Lovers

Map Legend

〔70〕	Interstate Highway	∧	Arch/Cave
〔550〕	US Highway	≍	Bridge
〔597〕	State Highway	■	Building/Point of Interest
〔7500〕〔FR591〕	County/Forest Road	▲	Campground
	Local Road	Ⅰ	Gate
= = = = = = =	Unpaved Road	P	Parking
- - - - - - -	Featured Trail	✕	Pass/Saddle
- - - - - -	Trail	▲	Peak
‖‖‖‖‖‖‖‖‖	Stairs/Ladder	◪	Scenic View/Viewpoint
- - - - - -	State Border	⌸	Tower
∼∼∼	Small River or Creek	○	Town/City
	Marsh/Swamp	①	Trailhead
	Body of Water	?	Visitor/Information Center
	National Forest/Park		
	National Monument/ Wilderness Area		

Best Hikes for Nature Lovers

13   Prater Ridge Trail: Mesa Verde National Park
16   Anasazi Arch Trail: Bureau of Land Management
18   Alien Run Trail: Bureau of Land Management
23   Bisti De-Na-Zin Wilderness: Bureau of Land Management
24   Bisti Badlands: Bureau of Land Management
28   Sipapu and Kachina Bridges Loop Trail: Natural Bridges National Monument
33   Corona Arch Trail: Bureau of Land Management

Arizona Region

Welcome to the Grand Canyon State! The northeastern Arizona portion of the Four Corners region is a vast and magnificent area filled with lofty buttes, towering cliffs, deep canyons, and spectacular blue skies. Most of the land is either Navajo or Hopi reservation. Both cultures have continued to take part in rich and ancient traditions that are centered on spiritual values, a connection to nature, and kinship. Driving through this region of the United States can feel a lot like traveling back in time, as many things have not changed for centuries. There are very few stores and restaurants in the smaller towns and villages that are scattered throughout the area. Visitors to the area will find themselves driving for many miles from town to town. It is important to be prepared with food and water, and be sure to fill up the gas tank whenever possible.

The highlights of the Arizona region include mesmerizing rock formations, enormous river-carved canyons, a dry and arid climate, ancient ruins, and fantastic mesas that have been carved out of this rugged and challenging landscape over many, many years. Seven of the trails in this book are found scattered throughout this vast area. In 2012 Arizona proudly boasted more than 10 million national park visits that resulted in almost $750 million in economic benefit for the state from its twenty-two National Park Service–managed lands. Only two of those national parks are included in this guide, but they offer some of the most spectacular views and scenery in northeastern Arizona. Canyon de Chelly National Monument and Navajo National Monument are both located on the Navajo Nation reservation and offer a few self-guided hikes as well as several guided hikes.

The other trails found in the Arizona region are in the Navajo Nation Parks and Recreation system. Park offices are located in Window Rock, Arizona. Window Rock is the capital of the Navajo Nation, the largest territory of a sovereign Native American nation in North America. There are seven units that are managed by the park system. This guide includes hikes in the Monument Valley Navajo Tribal Park, the Four Corners Monument, and the Lake Powell Navajo Tribal Park. These lands are very special and sacred to the Navajo people. Please respect and obey the rules and regulations that the land managers have implemented so that access to these beautiful places will continue. Hiking here seems to only be getting better!

◄ *View of Monument Valley from the trail (hike 2)*

1 White House Trail: Canyon de Chelly National Monument

The White House Trail offers hikers an amazing view of Canyon de Chelly and allows visitors a chance to experience what life was like several hundred years ago for the Puebloan people who inhabited the area. The 3-mile round-trip hike takes hikers from the canyon rim to the canyon floor to visit the White House Ruins and then back to the rim again.

Start: Southern end of the White House Overlook parking area
Distance: 3.0-mile out-and-back
Hiking time: 2 to 3 hours
Difficulty: Moderate due to gradual ascent on the return
Trail surface: Slickrock, sandy, and packed-dirt trail
Best season: Fall and spring

Other trail users: None
Canine compatibility: No dogs permitted
Fees and permits: No fees or permits required
Schedule: Open year-round
Maps: USGS: Chinle, AZ; park map and brochure available at the visitor center
Trail contact: Canyon de Chelly National Monument, PO Box 588, Chinle, AZ 86503; (928) 674-5500; www.nps.gov/cach

Finding the trailhead: From the Canyon de Chelly National Monument visitor center, drive 5.0 miles on South Rim Drive. Turn left (north) toward the White House Overlook and drive another 0.6 mile to the parking area. GPS: N36 7.830'/W109 28.655'

The Hike

It took millions of years of land uplifts and water erosion to create Canyon de Chelly. Because of the constant water flow, rich soil has continued to make its way into the canyon and has allowed for productive croplands and grazing for animals. The Ancient Puebloans who originally settled in the canyon built pit houses but eventually began to build their homes in the alcoves of the canyon walls to take advantage of the sunlight and natural protection. These people prospered until the mid-1300s; they eventually left the canyons to seek better farmlands.

President Herbert Hoover designated the canyon as a national monument in 1931. Today the monument covers about 84,000 acres on land within the Navajo Nation reservation and is still home to around forty families, many living in the canyon. The Park Service and the Navajo Nation work together to preserve the area, as it is a sacred place to the Navajo and holds much history. Local guiding services offer in-depth and informational tours into the canyon to those who are interested. The White House Trail is the only trail in the park that does not require a guide and is

White House Ruins

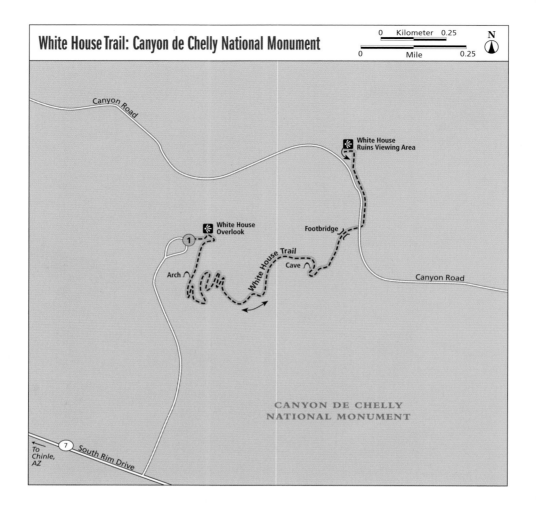

open to the public. The park does offer ranger-led hikes and activities, and there are even several overlooks located along the canyon rim that the public can drive to for views down into the canyon. Spider Rock Overlook is highly recommended before or after the hike.

The hike begins at the White House Overlook, about 6 miles from the visitor center. Locate the trailhead at the southern end of the overlook and parking area and begin hiking south on the slickrock along the canyon rim. There are excellent views all along the canyon rim, including a view of the White House Ruins before you leave for the hike and a great look east into the canyon at 0.1 mile. At 0.3 mile the trail turns left (east) and begins to descend into the canyon along the rocky and dirt-packed trail. There are several rock formations to check out and enjoy on the hike down the canyon wall, including a man-made cave at 1.0 mile.

Canyon de Chelly

Not long after passing through the cave, hikers will reach the canyon floor at 1.1 miles and will continue hiking north along the trail. There are some private property areas to respect along the canyon floor. At 1.2 miles you will cross over the Chinle Wash on a small footbridge and turn left (north) to continue toward the ruins. Reach the ruins at 1.5 miles. There is a fence here to keep people from entering the ruins, as they are a sacred place to the Navajo. Across the wash (southwest) are restrooms and a small recreation area where people can picnic and relax before the return hike. Return to the parking area and trailhead via the same route. Keep in mind that the hike back up the canyon wall can be strenuous for some people. Bring plenty of water and take advantage of the seating and rest areas during the hot summer months.

Miles and Directions

0.0 From the trailhead begin hiking south on the White House Trail.

0.1 Come to an overlook offering views east into the canyon.

0.3 The trail turns east and begins descending into the canyon.

1.0 The trail travels through a man-made cave.

1.1 Come to the canyon floor and continue hiking north.

1.2 Cross a small footbridge over Chinle Wash and then turn left (north).

1.5 Reach the White House Ruins viewing area. Retrace your steps to the trailhead.

3.0 Arrive back at the parking area after returning via the same route.

2 Wildcat Trail: Monument Valley Navajo Tribal Park

The Wildcat Trail is 4-mile lollipop hike into one of the most scenic areas that the Four Corners has to offer. Monument Valley has been the backdrop for a long list of films and television shows. This trail lets hikers feel like they stepped back in time into the Wild West. Hikers will travel around one of the "Mittens," a famous rock butte in the park, and will at one point find themselves standing in a spot where three towering buttes surround them.

Start: Wildcat Trail trailhead sign at the northwest corner of the visitor center parking area
Distance: 4.0-mile lollipop
Hiking time: 2 to 3 hours
Difficulty: Moderate due to sandy sections
Trail surface: Sand, dirt, and rock trail
Best season: Spring and fall
Other trail users: Horseback riders
Canine compatibility: Leashed dogs permitted

Fees and permits: Park entry fee required
Schedule: Open year-round; check website for closures
Maps: USGS: Rooster Rock, AZ-UT; trail map available at the park visitor center
Trail contact: Navajo Nation Parks and Recreation, PO Box 2520, Window Rock, AZ 86515; (928) 871-6647; http://navajonationparks.org/index.htm

Finding the trailhead: From Mexican Hat, Utah, drive west on US 163 for 20.5 miles to Monument Valley Road. Turn left (southeast) onto Monument Valley Road and drive 3.9 miles to the visitor center parking area and park in the northwest corner of the lot. The trailhead is just a short walk on Indian Route 42. GPS: N36 59.120'/W110 6.801'

The Hike

Monument Valley Navajo Tribal Park, known by the Navajo as Tse'Bii'Ndzisgaii, might be one of the most photographed places on earth. The valley is host to towering sandstone rock formations that have been sculpted over time and soar 400 to 1,000 feet above the valley floor. Combined with the surrounding mesas, buttes, and desert environment, it truly is one of the natural wonders of the world. The park covers almost 92,000 acres in northern Arizona and southern Utah, lies within the Navajo Nation reservation, and is managed by the Navajo Nation Parks and Recreation department.

Most have heard the basic science of an area like Monument Valley. Basically, over millions of years layers upon layers of sediments settled and cemented in a basin. The basin lifted up and became a plateau as the natural forces of wind and water slowly removed the softer materials and exposed what we see before us today. The spires, buttes, and other formations are still slowly chipping away but will be around long after we are gone. The formations in Monument Valley have become more and more famous as they have been seen in the backdrop of many movies and television shows, beginning with several John Wayne films. The visitor center offers museums,

Back side of the West Mitten

souvenirs, restrooms, a restaurant, a lodge, and much more. Guided tours of the park are available by vehicle and by horseback. The Wildcat Trail is the only self-guided trail in the park but offers some world-class scenery as it takes hikers for a walk through the world-famous Mitten Buttes and Merrick Butte.

After parking in the northwest section of the main parking area, walk north along Indian Route 42 for a short distance and follow the road as it turns right (east). The Wildcat Trail trailhead is at the northeast corner of the road intersection. Begin hiking north on the sandy trail as it slowly descends to the valley floor. The trail passes numerous rental cabins that face out toward the buttes as well, a great place to stay for the night. This section of the trail has some very sandy sections and may be a little challenging on the return hike. At 0.7 mile reach the loop portion of the hike and stay right (southeast) to follow the park's preferred direction of travel. The trail to the left (northeast) is the return trail.

As this portion of the hike begins, hikers will navigate through an area where the well-worn trail joins the wash and/or crosses the wash a time or two. Again, the trail is well worn and beginner navigation skills are all that is required. At 1.7 miles you will find yourself standing in the center of the two Mitten Buttes and Merrick Butte for a great panorama. Here the trail also joins a two-wheel-drive road for a short section. The road leads to private residences. At 1.8 miles veer left (northwest) off the

Wildcat Trail: Monument Valley Navajo Tribal Park

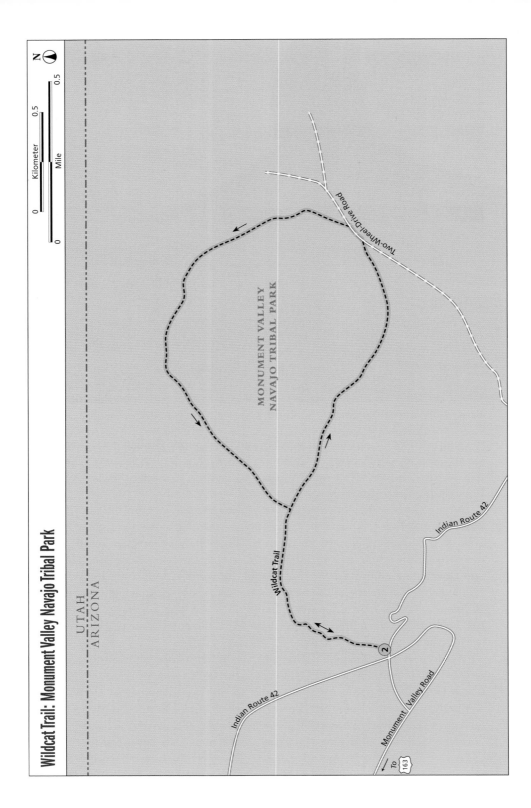

Wildcat Trail trailhead

road and back onto the narrow footpath. The trail continues along the valley floor through the desert shrublands and slowly circles northwest and then west around the westernmost Mitten Butte. The trail drops down into a large wash at 2.7 miles and continues in the wash for a short distance to 2.8 miles, where it exits the wash to the left (southwest). Hike up over a small hill and then back down to complete the loop portion of the hike at 3.3 miles. Turn right (west) to return to the trailhead and parking area via the same route at 4.0 miles.

Miles and Directions

- **0.0** Begin hiking north on the Wildcat Trail from the signed trailhead.
- **0.7** Stay right (east) at the junction to begin the loop portion of the hike. The trail to the left (northeast) is the return trail.
- **1.7** The trail joins a two-wheel-drive road for a short stretch while heading north.
- **1.8** Veer left (northwest) to leave the road and continue on the footpath.
- **2.7** The trail drops down into a wash. Continue hiking southwest in the wash.
- **2.8** Exit the wash to the left (southwest) and continue hiking on the narrow footpath.
- **3.3** Reach the end of the loop portion of the hike. Turn right (west) to return to the trailhead and parking area.
- **4.0** Arrive back at the trailhead and parking area.

Honorable Mentions

A Betatakin/Talastima Tour: Navajo National Monument

The Betatakin/Talastima Tour is located in the Navajo National Monument. Like many trails in the Navajo Nation reservation, the Betatakin/Talastima Tour requires a Navajo guide to hike the trail. Starting from the Tsegi Point Trail in the park, the round-trip guided hike is 5 miles and takes 3 to 5 hours to complete. The tour is free and is offered on a first-come, first-served basis. Call the number below to see if tours are currently running. To reach the trailhead, drive west from Kayenta, Arizona, on US 160 for about 19 miles. Turn right (north) onto AZ 564 and drive 9.4 miles. Turn left (west) onto Indian Route 221 and then make a quick right (north) to stay on Indian Route 221 for 0.9 mile to the visitor center and trailheads. For more information, for permits, or to obtain a trail map, contact Navajo National Monument, PO Box 7717, Shonto, AZ 86045; (928) 672-2700; www.nps.gov/nava/index.htm.

B Navajo National Monument Trails

Located in the Navajo National Monument, this 2.9-mile hike combines several of the park's trails to form an interesting day hike. From the visitor center hike the 0.8-mile out-and-back Canyon View Trail. Then hike east on the 1.3-mile out-and-back Sandal Trail to the Betatakin Overlook. On the return turn right (north) onto the 0.8-mile out-and-back Aspen Trail to complete your hike of all three trails. Highlights include great views of Betatakin and Fir Canyons. To reach the trailhead, drive west from Kayenta, Arizona, on US 160 for about 19 miles. Turn right (north) onto AZ 564 and drive 9.4 miles. Turn left (west) onto Indian Route 221 and then make a quick right (north) to stay on Indian Route 221 for 0.9 mile to the visitor center and trailheads. For more information, for permits, or to obtain a trail map, contact Navajo National Monument, PO Box 7717, Shonto, AZ 86045; (928) 672-2700; www.nps.gov/nava/index.htm.

C Rainbow Bridge Trail: Lake Powell Navajo Tribal Park

The 26-mile out-and-back Rainbow Bridge Trail is a must-do for desert hikers and natural bridge seekers. Rainbow Bridge spans about 275 feet, is 42 feet thick, and is about 33 feet wide. The trail to Rainbow Bridge is a road less traveled, as many people choose to view the bridge from a National Park Service viewing area or travel there by boat on Lake Powell. The trail is dry, dusty, and rugged and passes through several canyons en route to the bridge. A permit is required through the Navajo Nation Parks and Recreation system; call the number below. To reach the trailhead from Page, Arizona, drive east on AZ 98 about 45 miles to the Navajo Mountain Road turnoff. Turn left (north) and drive 33 miles. At the Navajo Mountain School sign, 6 miles from the trailhead, take the left fork. After 4 more miles you will come to a large sandstone knob, Haystack Rock. Take the right fork between the rock and Navajo Mountain and continue past War God Springs until your reach the ruins of a stone lodge. Once you pass War God Springs, the road becomes extremely rough and four-wheel drive is necessary. For more information, to check road and trail conditions, or to obtain a permit for the area, contact Navajo Nation Parks and Recreation, PO Box 2520, Window Rock, AZ 86515; (928) 871-6647; http://navajonationparks .org/index.htm.

D Upper Antelope Canyon: Lake Powell Navajo Tribal Park

The Navajo name for Upper Antelope Canyon is Tse'bighanilini, which translates to "the place where water runs through rocks." The canyon has become a destination for photographers and tourists from around the world. A guide service is required to enter the canyon as it is a special and sacred place to the Navajo. Some of the services require reservations, and others offer first-come, first-served tours. You will be driven to the canyon in the tour operator's vehicle and then allowed to explore. Call the Navajo Nation Parks and Recreation office at the number below for recommendations on a guide for this hike and directions to the guide service. For more information, to check road and trail conditions, or to obtain a permit for the area, contact Navajo Nation Parks and Recreation, PO Box 2520, Window Rock, AZ 86515; (928) 871-6647; http://navajonationparks.org/index.htm.

E Lower Antelope Canyon: Lake Powell Navajo Tribal Park

The Navajo name for Lower Antelope Canyon is Hasdeztwazi, which translates to "spiral rock arches." The canyon has become a destination for photographers and tourists from around the world. A guide service is required to enter the canyon as it is a special and sacred place to the Navajo. Some of the services require reservations, and others offer first-come, first-served tours. You will be driven to the canyon in the tour operator's vehicle and then allowed to explore. Call the Navajo Nation Parks and Recreation office at the number below for recommendations on a guide for this hike and directions to the guide service. For more information, to check road and trail conditions, or to obtain a permit for the area, contact Navajo Nation Parks and Recreation, PO Box 2520, Window Rock, AZ 86515; (928) 871-6647; http://navajo nationparks.org/index.htm.

Colorado Region

Welcome to Colorful Colorado! The southwestern Colorado portion of the Four Corners region is an awe-inspiring and diverse area filled with desert mesas, majestic mountains, deep canyons, and quaint mountain towns. Part of the land is Ute reservation, but a majority is public land. Mountain biking, ice climbing, mountaineering, whitewater rafting, kayaking, horseback riding, and of course hiking are just the start of a laundry list of things people can do in southwestern Colorado. Unlike in northeastern Arizona, there is a larger selection of stores and restaurants in the small towns that are scattered throughout the area, such as Cortez, Durango, Telluride, and Ouray.

Visitors to the area may find themselves driving and/or hiking at high elevations. The highest elevation for a hike in this region is over 14,000 feet. Driving over passes at 9,000 to 10,000 feet is not uncommon. Be prepared by drinking plenty of water before arriving and while in the area.

The highlights of the Colorado region include classic Rocky Mountains, enormous river-carved canyons, a dry and arid climate, ancient ruins, and fantastic mesas that have been carved out of this rugged and challenging landscape over eons. Eighteen of the trails in this book are scattered throughout this mountainous area. When people think of outdoor meccas in the lower forty-eight states, Colorado usually makes the list. However, many people tend to make their way to Denver because of the easier access via plane. Southwestern Colorado is a little tougher to get to but well worth the effort once you see how many fewer people there are. National parks in the area and included in this guide are Mesa Verde National Park, Hovenweep National Monument, and Canyons of the Ancients National Monument. Other parks nearby include the Black Canyon of the Gunnison National Park, Great Sand Dunes National Park, Colorado National Monument, and Chimney Rock National Monument.

Other trails in the Colorado region are located in Bureau of Land Management, National Forest Service, Colorado State, and City of Durango park systems. Hikers will find themselves in the canyons of western Colorado and along rivers that offer world-class trout fishing. They will follow historic trails like the Colorado Trail and walk up classic Colorado 14ers like Wilson Peak. Wilson Peak is often the advertising backdrop for companies like Jeep and Coors. Like many of the mountainous areas of Colorado, the southwest is known for its rich mining history. The lower elevations in the far southwest are scattered with old ruins including parks like Mesa Verde National Park, hosting some of the most notable and well-preserved ruins in the United States.

View from the summit of Engineer Mountain (hike 6)

3 Square Tower Trail: Hovenweep National Monument

The Square Tower Trail in Hovenweep National Monument is an excellent adventure for families. This 1.75-mile round-trip hike takes hikers for a short journey around the rim of Little Ruin Canyon and offers beautiful views of the ruins located in the canyon as well as of the surrounding area. Take advantage of one of few national park facilities that allows pets on the trails.

Start: To the south behind the visitor center
Distance: 1.75-mile lollipop
Hiking time: About 2 hours
Difficulty: Easy
Trail surface: Paved, packed-dirt, and slickrock trail
Best season: Fall through spring
Other trail users: None
Canine compatibility: Leashed dogs permitted

Fees and permits: Park entrance fee required at visitor center
Schedule: Open year-round
Maps: USGS: Negro Canyon, CO; trail map available in the park office
Trail contact: Hovenweep National Monument, McElmo Rte., Cortez, CO 81321; (970) 562-4282; www.nps.gov/hove/index.htm

Finding the trailhead: From Cortez, Colorado, turn west onto CR G and drive 29.8 miles to Reservation Road. Turn right (north) onto Reservation Road and drive 9.5 miles to Hovenweep Road. Turn right (east) onto Hovenweep Road/CR212 and drive 0.9 mile to Hovenweep Campground Road. Turn right (southeast) onto Hovenweep Campground Road/CR 268A and drive 0.3 mile to the visitor center and parking area. GPS: N37 23.142'/W109 4.517'

The Hike

Hovenweep National Monument is located on the border of Colorado and Utah, equidistant from the towns of Blanding, Utah; Bluff, Utah; and Cortez, Colorado. The remoteness of this park makes it an unlikely place to just stumble upon. Those who visit really want to be here, and they have good reason; the site's rich cultural history coupled with the raw, high desert beauty of the landscape make Hovenweep National Monument a worthy destination. The monument is also reliably less crowded than its neighbor to the east, Mesa Verde National Park, making it a good choice for folks hoping to escape busy trails.

According to park literature, humans have been visiting this area for more than 10,000 years. The first known people who used this land were nomadic hunters and gathers. Eventually people began to settle here. These people, known as Ancestral Puebloans, planted crops, including beans, corn, and squash, and built the towers found at this site between AD 500 and 1300, with the majority of the masonry being completed between AD 1200 and 1300. It seems that the site was abandoned by the end of the thirteenth century. Drought, warfare, and depletion of natural resources

Ruins on Square Tower Trail

are several of the hardships that historians and archaeologists believe encouraged the Ancestral Puebloans to leave this area.

The Square Tower Trail is an excellent choice for people wanting to view the unique tower-like ruins found in Hovenweep National Monument. Despite its relatively short distance, the Square Tower Trail visits many distinctive ruins and offers lovely desert scenery. The route begins just behind the visitor center and heads south along a paved walking trail. Along this portion of the trail, look for common plants of the Colorado Plateau, such as Mormon tea, Utah juniper, and cliff-rose. There are several interpretive signs pointing out and describing these plants. At 0.2 mile the paved portion of the trail ends at the rim of Little Ruin Canyon. Turn right (northwest) onto the dirt/rock path to hike the loop in a counterclockwise direction. After a very short distance, the trail passes a fortress-like ruin known as Stronghold House.

At 0.5 mile you come to a fork in the trail. Turn left (south) onto the Tower Point Loop Trail to visit the Tower Point Ruin. At Tower Point at 0.6 mile, enjoy great views of Little Ruin Canyon. Look just below the rim of the canyon to view several alcoves that were used by the Ancestral Puebloans to store crops. At 0.8 mile you will come to the ruin known as Hovenweep Castle, and shortly thereafter is a good view of Square Tower, a large, two-story ruin located down in the canyon. At 1.2 miles pass

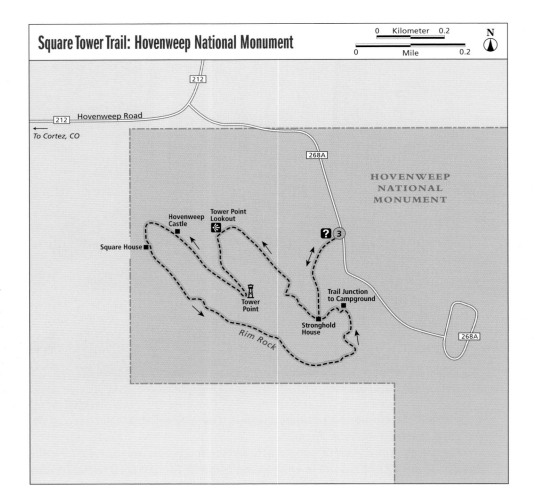

Square Tower Trail: Hovenweep National Monument

several more ruins before the trail curves to the north and descends into Little Ruin Canyon at 1.3 miles. Stay north and cross the canyon, coming to a trail junction at 1.5 miles shortly after reaching the north rim of the canyon. Turn left (northwest) to continue on the Square Tower Trail. The trail to the right (northeast) leads to the monument's campground. Shortly after the trail junction, the trail passes yet another ruin before coming to the end of the loop portion of the hike at 1.6 miles. Turn right (north) to return to the trailhead, visitor center, and parking area.

View of ruins and Sleeping Ute Mountain from Square Tower Trail

Miles and Directions

0.0   From the visitor center begin hiking south on the paved trail.

0.2   The paved trail ends at Little Ruin Canyon. Turn right (northwest) onto the dirt/rock path.

0.5   Turn left (south) onto the Tower Point Loop Trail.

0.6   Come to Tower Point.

1.3   The trail descends into Little Ruin Canyon.

1.5   Reach a trail junction. Stay left (northwest) to continue on Square Tower Trail. The trail to the right (northeast) goes to the campground.

1.6   Reach the end of the loop. Turn right (north) to return to the start.

1.75 Arrive back at the trailhead and visitor center.

4 Sand Canyon Trail: Canyons of the Ancients National Monument

The Sand Canyon Trail in the Canyons of the Ancients National Monument offers numerous recreational opportunities to locals as well as to visitors to the area. Hikers, bikers, and horseback riders all enjoy the 13.2-mile out-and-back trail and the surrounding area. Hikers choosing to explore this area will find numerous cliff dwellings located in Sand Canyon and will have beautiful views of Sleeping Ute Mountain on the return hike.

Start: Sand Canyon South Trailhead
Distance: 13.2-mile out-and-back
Hiking time: 7 to 8 hours
Difficulty: More challenging due to length
Trail surface: Dirt, rock, and sand trail
Best season: Fall through spring
Other trail users: Bikers and horseback riders
Canine compatibility: Leashed dogs permitted
Fees and permits: No fees or permits required

Schedule: Open year-round
Maps: USGS: Roggen, CO; trail map available at the Anasazi Heritage Center near Dolores, CO
Trail contact: Canyons of the Ancients National Monument and Anasazi Heritage Center, 27501 CO 184, Dolores, CO 81323; (970) 882-5600; www.blm.gov/co/st/en/nm/canm.html

Finding the trailhead: From Cortez, Colorado, drive 12.1 miles on CR G to the Sand Canyon South Trailhead and parking area on the right (north) side of the road. GPS: N37 20.494'/W108 49.066'

The Hike

The Canyons of the Ancients National Monument is overseen by the Bureau of Land Management and includes almost 171,000 acres of land in southwestern Colorado. The site has more than 6,000 recorded archaeological sites, and in some places there are as many as 100 sites per square mile. Researchers believe that several families came together around 1250 AD at the head of Sand Canyon and built a large, protective, U-shaped wall curving to the north, and then built hundreds of square rooms and round kivas within the wall. Community structures, plazas, and even a great kiva were built in this space. By 1275 AD it is believed that the Sand Canyon ruins were about three times the size of the Cliff Palace ruins that are found in Mesa Verde National Park. Not long after this prosperous growth came a series of events that ended the growth of Sand Canyon.

In 1276 a severe drought hit the area and caused many of the crops to fail and pushed most of the wildlife out of the area as well. Many of the residents suffered enough that they packed up and left for better living conditions. Still, many more stayed to live through the harsh conditions. Then, in 1277, it is believed that another

View of Sleeping Ute Mountain from Sand Canyon Trail

tribe attacked the people of Sand Canyon—probably a neighboring tribe that was suffering from the drought as well. The survivors from this attack packed up their belongings and moved on to other places. Native Americans from the area say that the spirits of the ancestors have been the only inhabitants of the ruins for more than 700 years. Many people travel to the monument today to bike ride, ride horses, and hike. The trail systems here allow for all three modes of travel, and most are marked to let people know which modes are allowed on each trail. There are no services at the trailhead, only a portable outhouse and an informational kiosk at the parking area.

Begin hiking north from the Sand Canyon South Trailhead and parking area over the slickrock trail that has been marked well with rock cairns. The trail circles around to the left (west) of a large rock formation and then reaches a side trail at 0.2 mile. To the right (east) the short trail leads to the first set of small ruins along the trail. Continue left (northeast) on the main trail as the slickrock ends at around 0.3 mile and the trail becomes a mix of sand and packed dirt. At 0.7 mile you will come to the first of several ruins of cliff dwellings. There are numerous sets of ruins along this route, and they will not all be pointed out in this guide as most are visible from the trail. Continue right (northeast) along the trail as it continues up the canyon. You will reach a trail junction at 1.7 miles. The trail to the left (west) connects to the East Rock Creek Trail; continue right (north) on the Sand Canyon Trail.

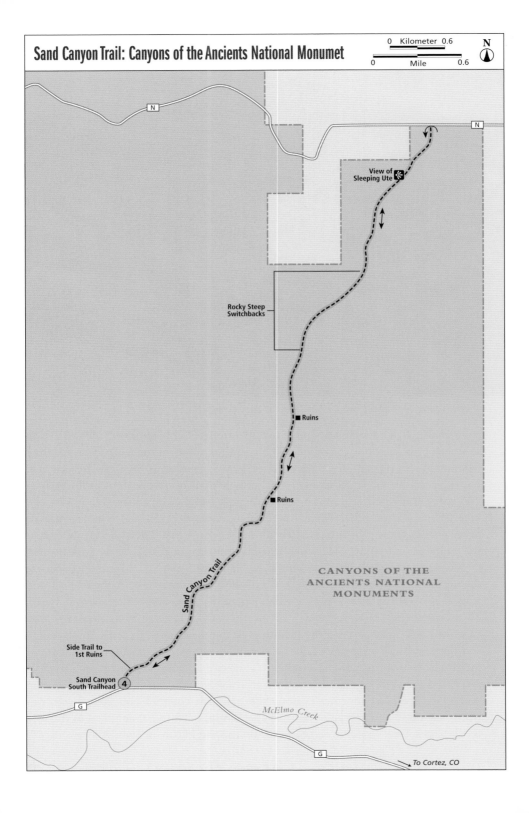

Sand Canyon Trail: Canyons of the Ancients National Monumet

0   Kilometer   0.6

0   Mile   0.6

N

N

N

View of
Sleeping Ute

Rocky Steep
Switchbacks

■ Ruins

■ Ruins

Sand Canyon Trail

CANYONS OF THE
ANCIENTS NATIONAL
MONUMENTS

Side Trail to
1st Ruins

Sand Canyon
South Trailhead   4

G

McElmo Creek

G

To Cortez, CO

Sand Canyon slowly narrows as you continue to hike north up into the canyon. At 3.6 miles you will see a sign that reads "Foot Traffic Only." The canyon becomes much narrower at this point, and you eventually reach a section of trail that begins switchbacking up the canyon wall on the west side of the canyon at 4.3 miles. A series of switchbacks will take you higher and higher up the canyon walls and will offer great views to the south of Sleeping Ute Mountain. Reach the end of the switchbacks at 5.1 miles and continue hiking north in what has now become a pine-forested area that provides a bit more shade. Hike through the beautifully forested high plains desert until you reach a steep climb at 6.4 miles. Hike up the steep hill, which includes a couple of switchbacks and then eventually flattens out as you arrive at the Sand Canyon North Trailhead at 6.6 miles. Turn around here and return to the Sand Canyon South Trailhead and parking area via the same route.

Miles and Directions

0.0 Begin hiking north from the Sand Canyon South Trailhead and parking area on the slick-rock trail marked with rock cairns.

0.2 Continue left (north) up the main trail. A trail to the right (east) leads to the first ruins.

0.3 The slickrock ends and the trail becomes sand and packed dirt.

0.7 Stay right (northeast); a trail to the left (northwest) leads to ruins.

1.7 Reach a trail junction with a connector trail that leads to the East Rock Creek Trail on the left (west). Continue hiking north on the Sand Canyon Trail.

3.6 Come to a sign that reads "Foot Traffic Only" as Sand Canyon begins to narrow.

4.3 Begin hiking up a series of switchbacks on the west side of the canyon.

5.1 Reach the top of the switchbacks and continue hiking north.

6.4 Hike up a steep section of trail.

6.6 Arrive at the Sand Canyon North Trailhead and parking area. Turn around here to return via the same route.

13.2 Arrive back at the Sand Canyon South Trailhead and parking area.

5 Rock of Ages Trail #429: Uncompahgre National Forest

The Rock of Ages Trail offers one of the more challenging and rewarding hikes in this guide. Hikers looking for an adventure and a physical challenge will enjoy this 9.2-mile out-and-back hike that not only leads to the 14,017-foot summit of Wilson Peak but also offers access to the 14,246-foot Mount Wilson and the 14,159-foot El Diente Peak. Some hikers opt to base camp at or near the Rock of Ages mine and hit all three peaks.

Start: Rock of Ages Trailhead and parking area
Distance: 9.2-mile out-and-back
Hiking time: 6 to 8 hours
Difficulty: More challenging due to steep climb (3,634 feet elevation gain) and rugged terrain; helmet is recommended
Trail surface: Forested path and rocky trail
Best season: Mid- to late summer
Other trail users: Horseback riders

Canine compatibility: Leashed dogs permitted
Fees and permits: No fees or permits required
Schedule: Open year-round
Maps: USGS: Mount Wilson, CO; National Geographic Trails Illustrated: #141
Trail contact: Grand Mesa, Uncompahgre, and Gunnison National Forests, 2250 US 50, Delta, CO 81416; (970) 874-6600; www.fs.usda .gov/main/gmug/home

Finding the trailhead: From Telluride, Colorado, drive 6 miles west on CO 145. Turn left onto the Silver Pick Road (CR 60M). Drive 4 miles to the intersection of CR 60M and CR 59H. Turn right onto CR 59H and continue south for 2.3 miles. Turn right at the Rock of Ages Trail sign onto FR 645. Proceed 2.2 miles to the Rock of Ages Trailhead. GPS: N37 52.989'/W108 1.109'

The Hike

Starting at 10,383 feet above sea level, the Rock of Ages Trail is a popular route for peak baggers looking to summit Wilson Peak, Mount Wilson, and El Diente Peak. These three 14ers all sit in the Lizard Head Wilderness in the San Juan and Uncompahgre National Forests. This hike description for the Rock of Ages Trail takes hikers to the summit of Wilson Peak. Yes, Wilson Peak is an official 14er, which puts it on many peak baggers' to-do list, but the peak has gained popularity with many other hikers because of the products it is used to endorse. The peak is found pictured on all Coors labels and products. Therefore, it is not uncommon to find "less experienced" hikers out on this more challenging trail because they have seen the mountain pictured in Coors or Jeep ads and just wanted to see it for themselves.

There are fifty-three 14ers in Colorado, and Wilson Peak is the forty-eighth highest. Even the two neighboring peaks are higher, with Mount Wilson at 14,246 feet and El Diente Peak at 14,159 feet. Wilson Peak is a great warm-up for the other two

Scree field on route to Wilson Peak

peaks, though, should you choose to check all three off in one trip. Believe it or not, some people hike to all three summits in one day. This trifecta has become known as "the Wilsons" to the peak-bagging community. Many of the hikes in this Four Corners guide are tough to get to, but this one might just take the cake. The nearest town is Telluride. If you've ever been to Telluride, then you already know just how difficult this area is as there is only one paved road into Telluride. You will have to work hard just to get to the trailhead for this hike and then work even harder to reach the summit. Remember, you are only halfway there once you reach the summit, and as many experienced mountaineers know, most accidents happen on the way down from the summit. Be sure to start early on this one, take plenty of food and water, carry layers, and don't be afraid to turn around if lightning storms roll in on you and your group.

From the Rock of Ages Trailhead and parking area, begin hiking south on the packed-dirt and forested trail. The trail begins a slow and steady climb up the mountain and passes the Wilson Mesa Trail on the right (west) at 0.1 mile. Continue hiking left (south) on the Rock of Ages Trail. The trail makes a few switchbacks up through the forest and eventually reaches another trail junction at 1.0 mile. To the right (south) is the Elk Creek Trail. Continue hiking to the left (southeast) as the dirt trail becomes rocky scree at 1.1 miles but returns to packed dirt shortly after. The trail continues northeast and circles around the ridge before turning southeast and then heading toward the Silver Pick Basin.

At 2.1 miles you will come to the first signed private property area. Stay right (south) on the trail and eventually pass through two private property gates that do allow access for hikers to pass through. The gates do not open and close; hikers simply go around them. Enter the Silver Pick Basin at 3.0 miles and come to the remains of an old rock house as the wide trail you've been hiking on becomes a narrow footpath. At the rock house look closely for rock cairns that lead east away from the house and then turn south again to continue up through the basin. At 3.2 miles the trail switchbacks up the right (west) side of the basin. After a few switchbacks the trail straightens and steadily climbs to the Rock of Ages saddle at 13,400 feet and 3.9 miles. Looking south, a trail leads down the other side of the saddle to the Rock of Ages mine. In the late 1800s much of this area was being mined for silver. A small wooden shelter stands there and many hikers use it as a resting point. At the saddle turn left (east) to begin your approach to Wilson Peak. (*Caution:* This next portion of the hike requires good balance and rock-scrambling skills. A helmet is recommended as well, as it is not uncommon to have other hikers above you knocking rocks loose.)

Hiking east from the Rock of Ages saddle, you will continue to follow the well-worn footpath as it traverses the south side of the mountain. At 4.1 miles you will reach a second saddle and turn left (northeast) again to begin traversing a very exposed section of trail. Use extreme caution on this section. There is no shame in scooting on your butt if you need to. After scrambling through this section, you reach the final challenging piece of the ascent at 4.5 miles. A long narrow ridge is in front of you. Don't be fooled here: You actually scramble down to the left (north) of the ridge and

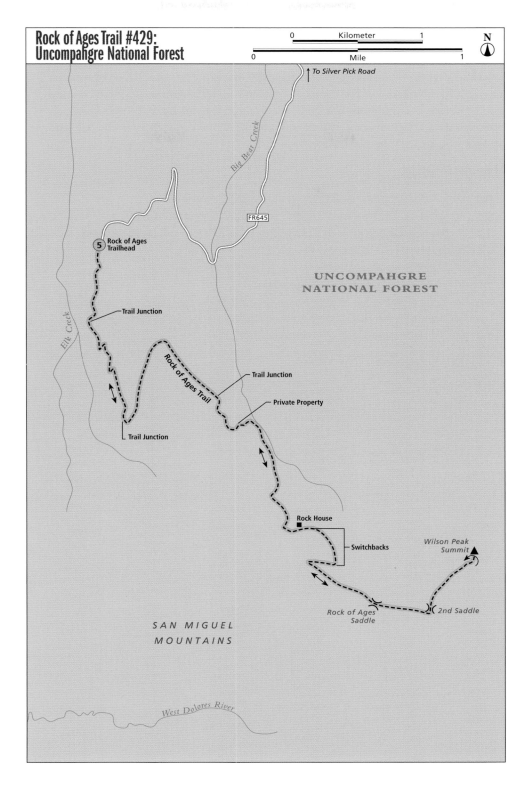

Kilometer

0   1

Mile

0   1

N

To Silver Pick Road

Big Bear Creek

FR645

Rock of Ages
Trailhead

5

UNCOMPAHGRE
NATIONAL FOREST

Elk Creek

Trail Junction

Rock of Ages Trail

Trail Junction

Private Property

Trail Junction

Rock House

Switchbacks

Wilson Peak
Summit

Rock of Ages
Saddle

2nd Saddle

SAN MIGUEL
MOUNTAINS

West Dolores River

cross over to climb back up on the other side. After the class 4 rock scramble, it's just a short walk to the summit at 4.6 miles. From the summit you can look to the south and southwest for beautiful views of Mount Wilson on the left and El Diente Peak on the right. The peaks are within 2 miles of the Wilson Peak summit and would require good physical conditioning or an extended trip to bag all three. Mount Wilson is considered the toughest climb and the most exposed. Turn and return to the trailhead and parking area via the same route.

Miles and Directions

0.0 Begin hiking south from the Rock of Ages Trailhead and parking area.

0.1 Stay left (south) on the Rock of Ages Trail; to the right (west) is the Wilson Mesa Trail.

1.0 Continue left (southeast) on Rock of Ages Trail; to the right (south) is the Elk Creek Trail.

1.1 The packed-dirt trail becomes rocky scree.

2.1 Stay right (south) on Rock of Ages Trail; to the left (east) is private property.

2.3 Pass through a couple of private property gates.

3.0 The trail becomes narrow as you enter the Silver Pick Basin. Watch for cairns that mark the trail to the east after passing the old rock house.

3.2 The trail switchbacks up the right (west) side of the basin.

3.9 Reach the first saddle and turn left (northeast). There are great views of the Rock of Ages mine to the south.

4.1 Reach the second saddle and turn left (northeast). The trail becomes class 3 and 4 rock scrambling.

4.5 Arrive at a long narrow ridge; scramble down to the left of the ridge and then hike back up.

4.6 Reach the summit of Wilson Peak. From here return to the trailhead via the same route.

9.2 Arrive back at the Rock of Ages Trailhead and parking area.

6 Pass Creek Trail to Engineer Mountain: San Juan National Forest

The Pass Creek Trail to Engineer Mountain summit is a Durango, Colorado, classic hike. Locals and visitors alike flock to this area in the summertime for first-time high-altitude experiences or to train for some of those Colorado 14ers. This 6.6-mile out-and-back hike takes hikers to almost 13,000 feet above sea level. The gradual ascent makes the hike ideal for first-timers. The network of trails in the area also attracts bikers and horseback riders.

Start: Pass Creek Trail parking area and trailhead

Distance: 6.6-mile out-and-back

Hiking time: 4 to 5 hours

Difficulty: More challenging due to rugged trail, elevation gain of 2,328 feet, and exposure

Trail surface: Forested and rocky trail

Best season: Mid- to late summer

Other trail users: Bikers and horseback riders

Canine compatibility: Leashed dogs permitted

Fees and permits: No fees or permits required

Schedule: Open year-round

Maps: USGS: Engineer Mountain, CO; National Geographic Trails Illustrated: #141

Trail contact: San Juan National Forest, 15 Burnett Ct., Durango, CO 81301; (970) 247-4874; www.fs.usda.gov/main/sanjuan/home

Finding the trailhead: From Durango, Colorado, drive about 37 miles north on US 550. At the top of Coal Bank Pass (just past the Coal Bank Pass pullout on the right), turn left (west) onto a small dirt road. Drive about 50 yards to the Pass Creek Trail parking area and trailhead. GPS: N37 41.951'/W107 46.743'

The Hike

Engineer Mountain is a distinctive and prominent peak that stands tall above the Animas Valley to those driving north from Durango on US 550. In fact, it might be one of the most photographed peaks in the San Juans. The peak is a very high 12er and oftentimes is mistaken for a 13er. The peak rises high to the southwest of the historic mining town of Silverton, and the trail for this hike is accessed from Coal Bank Pass on the way from Durango to Silverton or vice versa. What makes this mountain seem so big and causes it to be mistaken for a 13er or 14er is that the summit has nearly 1,500 feet of vertical prominence and, according to most, the visual prominence to match the numbers.

The easy access to the trail from US 550 makes Engineer Mountain a great option for a half-day outing in the summer. The fact that the highway is plowed in the winter also makes it an option for those looking to practice their winter backcountry travel skills. The rest area at Coal Bank Pass provides restrooms for before and after the hike. The hike from the Pass Creek Trailhead to the Engineer Mountain summit provides

Alpine meadow along Pass Creek Trail

an amazing array of wildflowers in the late spring and summer months. Be aware that the first 1.5 miles of the trail is in forest, making the early- and late-spring hiking seasons a little more challenging due to snow cover.

Locate the Pass Creek Trailhead and parking area just after the Coal Bank Pass parking area and begin hiking north on the Pass Creek Trail. The trail begins by passing through an open meadow as it heads toward a pine tree forest. Reach the forest at 0.3 mile and, depending on the time of year, perhaps hop over a few snow runoffs. The trail is well worn and easy to navigate through the forest. At 0.6 mile you'll reach a short series of switchbacks and follow the trail as it begins turning west. A small pond at 1.2 miles is a great spot to rest if you are still getting used to the elevation. It is not uncommon to see a few tents set up in the area as well. Be sure to check with the Forest Service about camping regulations in the area.

Continue hiking uphill gradually after leaving or passing the pond. After a few more switchbacks and then an enjoyable stroll through the rest of the forested section of the trail, the forest ends and the trail leads out into a beautiful open meadow. In the spring and summer, the wildflower show is spectacular here! In the meadow you will come to a trail junction at 2.5 miles; stay right (northwest) to begin your approach up toward the Engineer Mountain summit. The trail becomes much steeper from here and begins following a ridge up the mountain. At 2.9 miles the packed-dirt trail

Pass Creek Trail to Engineer Mountain: San Juan National Forest

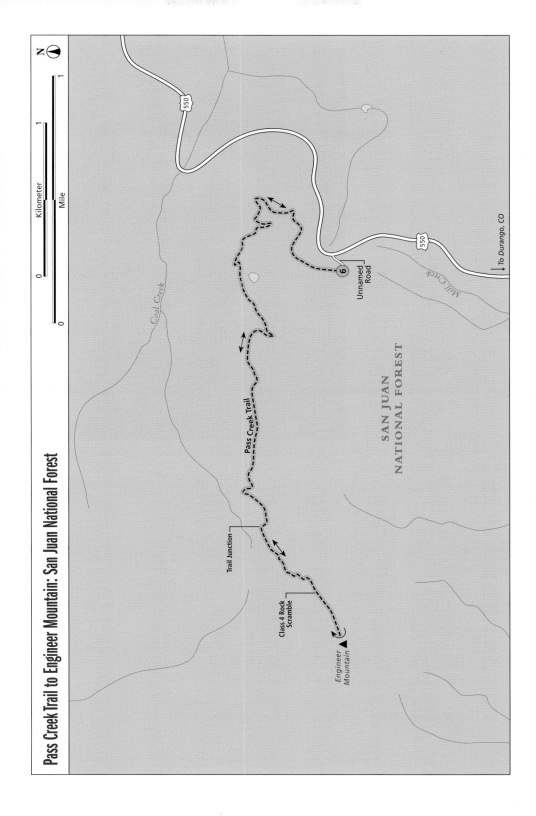

ends and the trail becomes rocky scree. Continue up the ridge to the toughest section of the hike. Some class 4 rock scrambling will be required here to climb up through a narrow slot and then traverse a section of trail that is very exposed to the southeast. Once you have navigated your way through this section, it is just a short walk to the top. You'll reach the summit of Engineer Mountain (12,973 feet) at 3.3 miles. After soaking in the views, turn and return to the trailhead and parking area via the same route. (**Caution:** If you have never hiked at high altitudes, be sure to bring plenty of food and water and layers for unexpected weather. Take your time as your body adjusts to the thinner air, and never

Class 4 rock scrambling near summit of Engineer Mountain

be scared to turn around when lightning storms come rolling in. You can always come back and try again.)

Miles and Directions

0.0 Begin hiking north on the Pass Creek Trail from the parking area.

0.3 After crossing a meadow, enter a pine tree forest.

0.6 Reach a short series of switchbacks and begin hiking west.

1.2 Come to a small pond and an excellent place to sit and relax for snacks.

2.5 Reach a trail junction. Stay right (northwest) to begin the approach to Engineer Mountain.

2.9 The packed-dirt trail ends and the trail becomes rocky scree.

3.0 Reach a section that requires class 4 rock scrambling.

3.3 Arrive at the summit. Return via the same route.

6.6 Arrive back at the Pass Creek Trail parking area and trailhead.

7 Spud (Potato) Lake Trail #661: San Juan National Forest

Known by locals as Spud Lake, Potato Lake is a great family adventure. Be sure to grab a fishing pole (and permit) for this hike. Potato Lake offers beautiful mountain scenery at a high-altitude fishing pond. The lake sits at the base of Spud Mountain and gives hikers hours upon hours of hiking, exploring, fishing, and relaxing options.

Start: Spud (Potato) Lake Trailhead and parking area north of the lily pad–covered lake
Distance: 2.4-mile out-and-back
Hiking time: 2 to 3 hours
Difficulty: Moderate due to the length of the trail
Trail surface: Forested trail
Best season: Any

Other trail users: Horseback riders
Canine compatibility: Leashed dogs permitted
Fees and permits: No fees or permits required
Schedule: Open year-round
Maps: USGS: Engineer Mountain, CO
Trail contact: San Juan National Forest, 15 Burnett Ct., Durango, CO 81301; (970) 247-4874; www.fs.usda.gov/main/sanjuan/home

Finding the trailhead: From Durango, Colorado, drive about 28.5 miles north on US 550 and turn right (south) onto FR 591/Lime Creek Road. Drive 2.9 miles to a parking area on the left (north) side of the road. GPS: N37 39.161'/W107 46.409'

The Hike

The San Juan National Forest is southwestern Colorado's gateway to adventure and includes approximately 1.8 million acres of federal lands that are managed by the U.S. Forest Service. There is an amazing range of scenery in this part of the Four Corners region. Near the actual Four Corners, Colorado consists of high desert mesas and canyons, and as you travel east into the state, you will encounter majestic alpine peaks and meadows. The San Juan National Forest features a national forest scenic byway, the San Juan Skyway Scenic Byway, and a Bureau of Land Management four-wheel-drive scenic byway, the Alpine Loop Backcountry Byway. Visitors come here for the same reason that the locals live here: They can enjoy a variety of outdoor activities including hiking, mountain biking, hunting, fishing, skiing, horseback riding, and camping. The San Juan National Forest also shares management duties of three designated wilderness areas: the Weminuche Wilderness, the Lizard Head Wilderness, and the South San Juan Wilderness.

You will see many maps and other guides refer to this trail as the Potato Lake Trail. Because the Forest Service web page refers to it as Spud Lake Trail, we will also refer to it as Spud Lake Trail in this guide.

Once you've located the unsigned parking area on the north side of FR 591/Lime Creek Road and directly north of a decent-sized lily pad–covered lake, begin

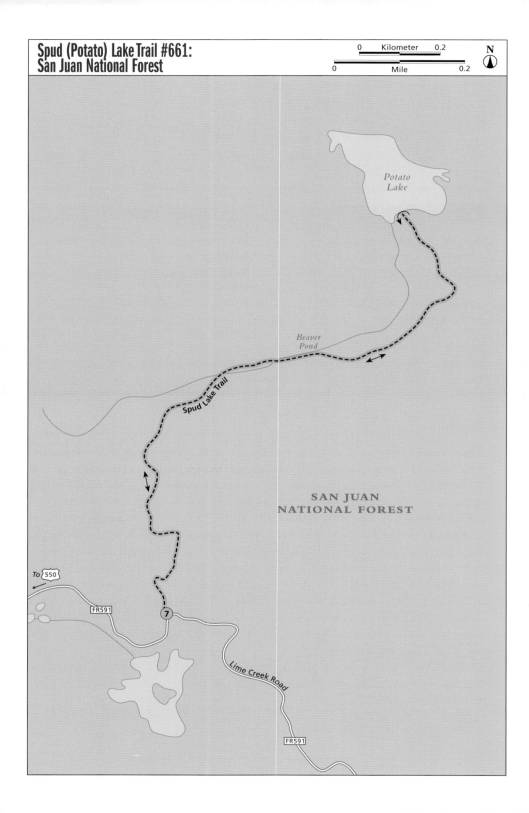

Kilometer

Mile

N

Potato
Lake

Beaver
Pond

Spud Lake Trail

SAN JUAN
NATIONAL FOREST

To 550

FR591

7

Lime Creek Road

FR591

Lily pad–covered lake near Spud Lake Trailhead

hiking north on the packed-dirt and rocky trail to the northeast of the parking area. The trailhead is at approximately 9,400 feet, and the trail will gain about 400 vertical feet once you've arrived at Spud Lake. Hiking north, you will pass through a beautiful aspen grove as the trail gradually climbs the uphill grade and levels out for a short distance at 0.3 mile. At 0.5 mile begin the gradual climb again as the trail becomes a bit rockier and then passes a beaver pond on the left (north) at 0.7 mile. Continue hiking east and then north as the trail finishes up its last uphill and arrives at Spud Lake at 1.2 miles with Potato Hill looming in the background. After a little fishing, relaxing, or a stroll around the lake, return to the trailhead and parking area via the same route.

Miles and Directions

0.0 Begin hiking north on the rocky trail just east of the parking area.

0.3 After heading gradually uphill through an aspen grove, the trail begins to level out.

0.5 The trail begins a gradual climb again.

0.7 Pass a small beaver pond on the left (north).

1.2 Arrive at Potato (Spud) Lake. Return to the trailhead and parking area via the same route.

2.4 Arrive back at the trailhead and parking area.

8 Purgatory Trail #511: San Juan National Forest

This 3.8-mile out-and-back trail takes hikers through beautiful aspen groves down to an area known as Purgatory Flats. Once at the Flats, hikers can enjoy time along Cascade Creek or extend their hike on the Animas River Trail. This area is also a popular place for bird-watching and offers a great fall foliage hike through the aspens.

Start: Purgatory Trail trailhead on the south side of Tacoma Drive
Distance: 3.8-mile out-and-back
Hiking time: 2 to 3 hours
Difficulty: Moderate due to length and rugged terrain
Trail surface: Forested trail and dirt path
Best season: Fall from Sept to Nov for the fall foliage

Other trail users: Horseback riders
Canine compatibility: Leashed dogs permitted
Fees and permits: No fees or permits required
Schedule: Open year-round
Maps: USGS: Engineer Mountain, CO; National Geographic Trails Illustrated: #140 and #144
Trail contact: San Juan National Forest, 15 Burnett Ct., Durango, CO 81301; (970) 247-4874; www.fs.usda.gov/main/sanjuan/home

Finding the trailhead: From Durango, Colorado, drive about 26.5 miles north on US 550 and turn right (south) onto Tacoma Drive. Drive 0.2 mile on Tacoma Drive to a parking area on the left (north) side of the road. GPS: N37 37.780' / W107 48.392'

The Hike

The Purgatory Trail is a great day-trip trail that winds down through a beautiful aspen forest and then pops out alongside Cascade Creek. The area down in the valley is a popular place for overnight camping or makes a great rest stop for hikers out on a longer journey. The trail begins directly across from the entrance to the Durango Mountain Resort, a beautiful place to spend the night if you are staying in the area. The resort is a great base camp for those looking to "camp" in style while enjoying everything that the area has to offer, including world-class mountain biking, world-class trout fishing, hiking and camping, and the Million Dollar Highway, the section of US 550 from Silverton to Ouray. The trail drops quickly to Purgatory Flats, an open grassy valley 1 mile below the highway. Purgatory Flats is a historical grazing area, so don't be surprised to see cattle down in the valley when you arrive. You'll want to get a fishing permit and bring your rod and reel for this one if you fish. Lime Creek and Cascade Creek converge here and offer good trout fishing.

From the trailhead on the south side of Tacoma Drive, begin hiking southeast on the packed-dirt and rocky trail. At 0.1 mile you will reach the Weminuche Wilderness

Early fall on Purgatory Trail ▶

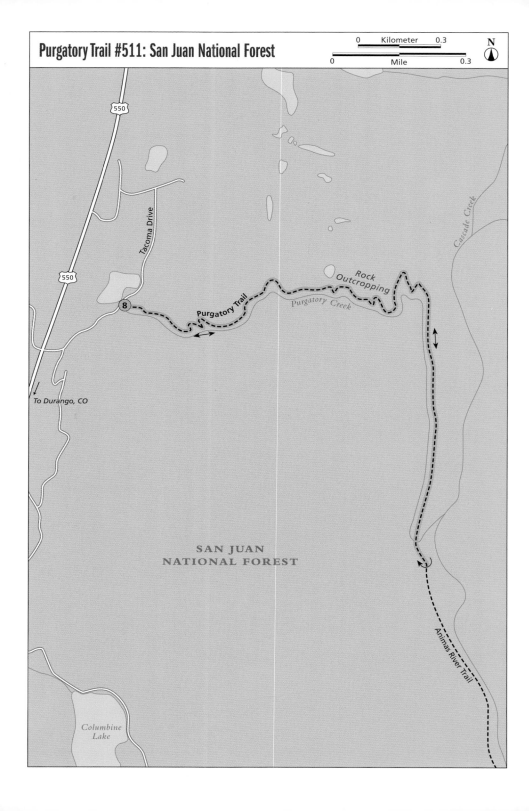

Purgatory Trail #511: San Juan National Forest

0   Kilometer   0.3

0   Mile   0.3

N

550

Tacoma Drive

550

Cascade Creek

Rock Outcropping

Purgatory Trail

Purgatory Creek

8

To Durango, CO

SAN JUAN
NATIONAL FOREST

Animas River Trail

Columbine
Lake

Purgatory Trailhead

kiosk and trail register. Be sure to register yourself and your group, as it helps the land managers track usage and could be used to help track you should you get lost. Continue hiking southeast from the register as the trail begins its descent down the west side of the valley wall. Come to a small but easily rock-hopped creek crossing at 0.4 mile. The trail continues to descend through a beautiful aspen grove. Time your hike just right in the fall, and you are in for quite a treat, as this entire area is known for its fall foliage beauty.

At 0.9 mile the trail circles south to a great little overlook area that provides views south down toward Cascade Canyon. The trail continues its half circle so that you are hiking north for a short distance before coming to a short series of switchbacks that will finish the descent and end at the valley floor at 1.2 miles. This descent was by no means the steepest one in the area or in this guide, but don't let it fool you, and remember that you'll need the energy to hike back up on the way back. Once on the valley floor, you can see a few camping areas to the east and north in the forested areas of the Flats. Continue hiking south on the Purgatory Trail out onto the Purgatory Flats. Arrive at a great rest area along Cascade Creek just before entering Cascade Canyon at 1.9 miles. Though the trail continues for several miles south into the canyon, this is the turnaround point for this hike description.

Miles and Directions

0.0   Locate the trailhead on the south side of Tacoma Drive and begin hiking south.

0.1   Come to the Weminuche Wilderness kiosk and trail register.

0.4   Reach a small creek crossing.

0.9   Reach a nice overlook area on the right that looks down into Purgatory Flats.

1.2   The descent ends, and you arrive at the Flats.

1.9   Arrive at Cascade Creek. Return to the trailhead and parking area via the same route.

3.8   Arrive back at the trailhead and parking area.

9 Animas Mountain Trail: City of Durango

The Animas Mountain Trail is a convenient 5.8-mile loop for which the trailhead is located within the city limits of Durango. Popular with locals, this trail offers a quick getaway from the city without the long drive to and from the trailhead. The trail rises high above Durango and offers beautiful views of the city to the south and the Animas Valley to the north.

Start: Animas Mountain Trailhead and parking area

Distance: 5.8-mile loop

Hiking time: 3 to 4 hours

Difficulty: Moderate due to modest climbs

Best season: Spring through fall

Other trail users: Bikers

Canine compatibility: Leashed dogs permitted

Fees and permits: No fees or permits required

Schedule: Open year-round

Maps: USGS: Durango West, CO

Trail contact: Tres Rios Field Office, 29211 CO 184, Dolores, CO 81323; (970) 882-7296; www.blm.gov/co/st/en/fo/sjplc.html

Finding the trailhead: From downtown Durango, Colorado, drive north 1.8 miles on Main Avenue. Turn left (west) onto West 32nd Street and drive 0.2 mile. Turn right (north) onto West 4th Avenue and drive 0.1 mile to the trailhead and parking area. GPS: N37 18.173'/W107 52.362'

The Hike

Because of its great access, beautiful Animas Valley views, and gradual uphill grade, this 5.8-mile loop on the Animas City Mountain is a local favorite and ideal warm-up for visitors to the area before hitting the big peaks. The trail travels along the eastern rim through a pinyon-juniper and scrub oak forest for the first section of the hike, offers spectacular views of the San Juan Mountains, and then snakes its way through a ponderosa forest on the western side of the mountain before returning to the city. There is a small network of trails on the mountain that offer numerous trip options—this description is for the largest loop. The Animas City Mountain is managed by the Bureau of Land Management and is subject to occasional closures due to weather, fires, and wildlife. There are trail maps along the trail to help keep you en route.

Begin hiking north from the parking area and trailhead sign. At 0.1 mile turn right (northeast) to begin hiking up a short series of switchbacks. The trail switchbacks up through a landscape of pinyon-juniper and scrub oak. As you hike up the eastern rim of the mountain, you will come to a few trail junctions. At each of the three junctions, bear right (northeast) to continue up the eastern rim. Turning left (west) onto any of these trails will loop you back down the mountain to the trailhead and parking area. The most obvious trail junctions are at 0.7 mile, 1.8 miles, and 2.2 miles. You'll also pass several overlooks on the right (east) as you hike up the mountain that offer great views of the Animas Valley and the Animas River.

View of San Juan Mountains from the Animas Mountain Trail

At approximately 2.7 miles there's a short, gradual climb northwest to the summit of Animas Mountain at 8,161 feet. From there the trail continues a short distance west before making a sharp left turn south to begin a gradual descent down the western side of the mountain. Fabulous views of the La Plata Mountains can be had as you travel down this side of Animas Mountain. Silver Mountain is the highest peak on the left. The trail is packed dirt at first but then gets rocky as you descend. At the 5.3-mile mark you are faced with the first of four left (east) turn options. Stay right (southwest) to continue on the main trail past the first three turns. At 5.6 miles the trail makes a sharp left turn to the east. Turn here to make your return to the trailhead; the right-hand (south) path leads to another trail access and parking area. Continue down a few short switchbacks and then turn right (south) to return to the trailhead and parking area.

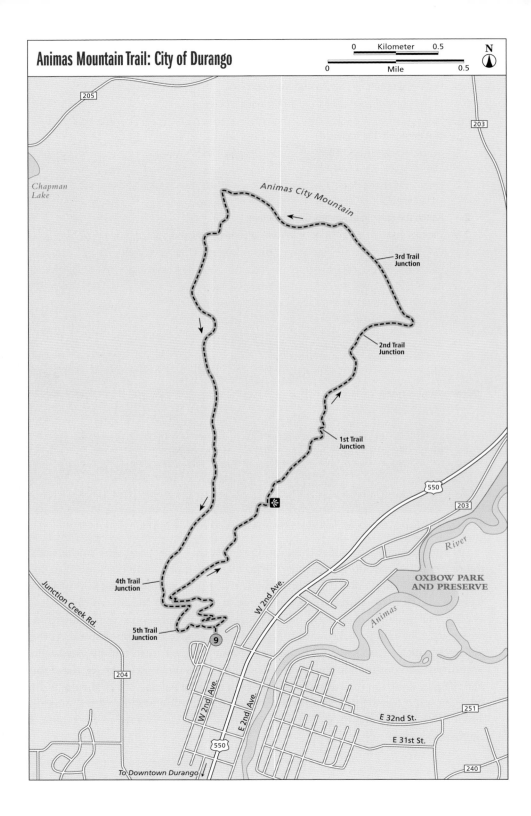

Animas Mountain Trail: City of Durango

Animas City Mountain

Chapman
Lake

3rd Trail
Junction

2nd Trail
Junction

1st Trail
Junction

Junction Creek Rd.

4th Trail
Junction

5th Trail
Junction

9

OXBOW PARK
AND PRESERVE

River

Animas

W 2nd Ave.

W 2nd Ave.

E 2nd Ave.

E 32nd St.

E 31st St.

To Downtown Durango

205

203

550

203

204

251

550

240

0   Kilometer   0.5

0   Mile   0.5

N

Miles and Directions

0.0   Begin hiking north on the Animas Mountain Trail.

0.1   Turn right (northeast) to hike the trail counterclockwise.

0.7   Stay right (northeast) to continue on the main trail; to the left (northwest) is a shorter loop that returns to the trailhead.

1.8   Stay right (northeast) to continue on the main trail; to the left (northwest) is a shorter loop that returns to the trailhead.

2.2   Continue right (northwest) at the trail junction; the left (south) path returns to the trailhead.

2.7   Reach the summit of Animas City Mountain.

2.9   The trail makes a sharp left (south) turn and begins descending.

5.3   Stay right (south) to continue on the main trail; to the left (east) is a social trail.

5.6   Turn left (east) to return to the trailhead; the trail to the right (south) goes to another trail access and parking area.

5.7   Turn right (south) to return to the trailhead and parking area.

5.8   Arrive back at the start.

Animas Mountain Trailhead

10 Colorado Trail: Southern Terminus Trailhead to Quinn Creek

Welcome to the southern terminus of the Colorado Trail! This 5.4-mile out-and-back section of the trail will give all the thru-hike dreamers a small taste of what the trail has to offer. The trail travels along Junction Creek and offers numerous areas to enjoy the nice cool mountain runoff during the warm mountain summer days.

Start: Colorado Trail Durango trailhead and parking area

Distance: 5.4-mile out-and-back

Hiking time: About 3 hours

Difficulty: Moderate due to length and some steep climbs

Trail surface: Forested trail

Best season: Spring through fall

Other trail users: Bikers and horseback riders

Canine compatibility: Leashed dogs permitted

Fees and permits: No fees or permits required

Schedule: Open year-round

Maps: USGS: Durango West, CO; trail map available at www.coloradotrail.org

Trail contact: San Juan National Forest, 15 Burnett Court, Durango, CO 81301; (970) 247-4874; www.fs.usda.gov/sanjuan

Finding the trailhead: From Durango, Colorado, drive north on Main Avenue for 1.1 miles. Turn left (west) onto West 25th Street. Continue 0.2 mile on West 25th Street until a slight right and the road becomes Junction Street. Drive 0.9 mile on Junction Street and then stay left onto CR 204/Junction Creek Road. After 2.5 miles turn left (west) into the parking area and trailhead. GPS: N37 19.882'/W107 54.176'

The Hike

The Colorado Trail is an idea that was conceived back in 1973 by Bill Lucas and Merrill Hastings. Since that time the trail has become an established, marked, and mostly non-motorized trail open to hikers, horse riders, and bicyclists. From Waterton Canyon near Denver, the trail makes its way for almost 500 miles from the Front Range over the Rockies, through the state's most mountainous regions, to the outskirts of Durango. Thru-hikers taking on the entire trail will pass through eight mountain ranges, six national forests, and six wilderness areas. Trail elevations range from about 5,500 feet at Denver to a high of 13,271 feet in the San Juan Mountains.

Passing through some of the state's most beautiful country, the trail allows an abundance of wildlife and wildflower viewing and photography. In addition to offering stunning natural scenery, the trail also passes through historic mining towns, ski resorts, and quaint mountain towns. The western portion of the trail tends to see less

Quinn Creek

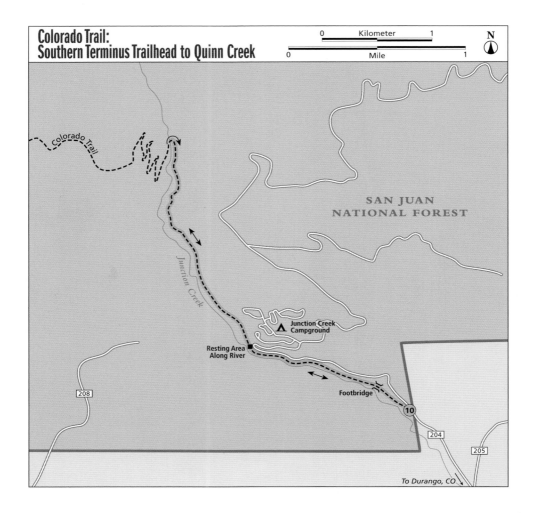

Colorado Trail:
Southern Terminus Trailhead to Quinn Creek

SAN JUAN
NATIONAL FOREST

Junction Creek
Campground

Resting Area
Along River

Footbridge

To Durango, CO

human impact, as this side of the mountains and the Four Corners area continue to be more challenging to reach by plane and vehicle. The southern terminus section described here does not give hikers a good feel for the high-altitude hiking one would experience on other sections of the trail, but the beautiful scenery and the opportunity to just get your feet on the trail is enough to get serious hikers thinking about the possibilities of a thru-hike.

From the Colorado Trail trailhead and parking area, begin hiking northwest on the packed-dirt trail. The trailhead area has a pit toilet that closes in the late fall and may still be closed in early spring. There is also a nice information kiosk at the trailhead for those interested in the information or, more importantly, the photo op. For the entire section described here, the trail parallels Junction Creek until the turnaround point at Quinn Creek. At 0.2 mile cross a small footbridge over a drainage that runs into Junction Creek and continue hiking northwest. The trail begins a slow and gradual climb on the right (north) side of the valley and passes numerous areas to stop and enjoy the cool waters of Junction Creek. At mile 1.1 is a great place to pull off to the left side of the trail and sit by the creek or even cool your feet during those warm summer months.

Continue hiking northwest on the trail from here and reach another trail access point on the right (north) at 1.2 miles. The forest is thick with ponderosa pine, fir, and spruce trees. There is a parking area, a trail kiosk, and access to the Junction Creek Campground just up the road from this point. The Junction Creek Campground is a great base camp for those looking to spend a few days in the area. The campground has forty-four sites, outhouses, and picnic facilities. The site is managed by the Forest Service. The road to the campground does close in the winter, so check its website for that information. From here continue hiking as the trail continues on an uphill grade until 2.3 miles into the hike, where the trail then descends to the Junction Creek bridge. Reach the bridge at 2.7 miles. Hikers can cross the bridge and continue as the trail moves into a series of switchbacks. The description for this hike ends at the bridge. Turn here and return to the trailhead and parking area for a 5.4-mile outing.

Miles and Directions

0.0 Begin hiking northwest on the Colorado Trail.

0.2 Cross a small wooden footbridge.

1.1 Come to a nice rest area on the left (south) side of the trail with great creek access.

1.2 Pass another parking area and trail access point on the right (north).

2.3 After a short ascent, the trail begins descending to the creek.

2.7 Arrive at the Junction Creek bridge. Turn around here to return to the start.

5.4 Arrive back at the parking area and trailhead.

11 Animas River Trail: City of Durango

The Animas River Trail stretches nearly 7 miles through Durango and continues to develop as the city develops. This 7-mile out-and-back section is a great family adventure and offers several access points to the many attractions in downtown Durango.

Start: Memorial Park Trailhead and parking area
Distance: 7.0-mile out-and-back
Hiking time: 4 to 5 hours
Difficulty: Moderate due to length
Trail surface: Paved trail
Best season: Any
Other trail users: Bikers

Canine compatibility: Leashed dogs permitted
Fees and permits: No fees or permits required
Schedule: Open year-round
Maps: USGS: Durango East, CO
Trail contact: City of Durango, 949 E. 2nd Ave., Durango, CO 81301; (970) 375-5000; www.durangogov.org/index.aspx?NID=568

Finding the trailhead: From downtown Durango, Colorado, drive 1.8 miles on Main Avenue. Turn right (east) onto East 32nd Street and drive 0.2 mile. Turn right (south) onto East 3rd Avenue and drive 0.3 mile before turning right (south) onto Rio Vista Circle. Continue 0.2 mile on Rio Vista Circle before arriving at the Memorial Park parking area and trailhead. GPS: N37 17.701'/W107 52.199'

The Hike

The city of Durango offers everything you'd expect to find in a Colorado mountain town and more. Founded in 1880, Durango was developed to serve the mining community that continued to grow in the area. Silver was being mined farther north in towns like Silverton, but the weather there was so harsh and the water and coal was so much more plentiful around Durango that the mining companies found it more affordable to set up their smelters here and move material to Durango. Around 2,400 people, mostly miners, were living in Durango when it was founded. The creation of the San Juan National Forest and designation of Mesa Verde National Park in 1905 and 1906 aided in a population boom, and by 1910 there were close to 5,000 people living in Durango and many more people were starting to make their way here for vacations. Today the population numbers around 14,000 people.

The city is home to Fort Lewis College, a four-year university that was once a boarding school for Native Americans. Tourist attractions include things like the Durango and Silverton Narrow Gauge Railroad, the Durango Mountain Resort, festivals like the Snowdown Festival, natural features like the Animas River Valley, and of course a historic downtown Main Street. Visitors come to Durango for mountain biking, rock climbing, skiing, snowboarding, kayaking, rafting, road biking, trail

Trail passes the dog park and the whitewater park

running, fishing, horseback riding, and of course hiking. The ATV community finds numerous things to do in this ATV-friendly area as well. There is no shortage of rough mountain roads to drive on and see how far your vehicle can make it before needing to turn around. With all that there is to offer in and around Durango, the locals and visitors both continue to flock to the oh-so-popular Animas River Trail, where many of the activities above take place, especially hiking.

From the Memorial Park parking area and trailhead, begin hiking south on the paved trail at the southwest corner of the lot. Bikers, hikers, walkers, runners, and tubers all use the path on a regular basis. The trail follows closely along the Animas River as it flows south and cuts right through the middle of the city. At 0.3 mile cross a bridge over the river and then cross the train tracks before turning left (south) to continue hiking south. You'll come to another trail access point at 0.7 mile. Turn left (south) to stay on the trail. At 1.2 miles you will arrive at Rotary Park, one of several great parks along the trail that offer spaces to sit and relax. Stay right (west) to continue on the trail through Rotary Park; heading left (south) takes you off the trail.

The trail continues to follow along the river as it strays away from the main downtown area by circling west around the downtown. Cross another bridge at 1.7 miles

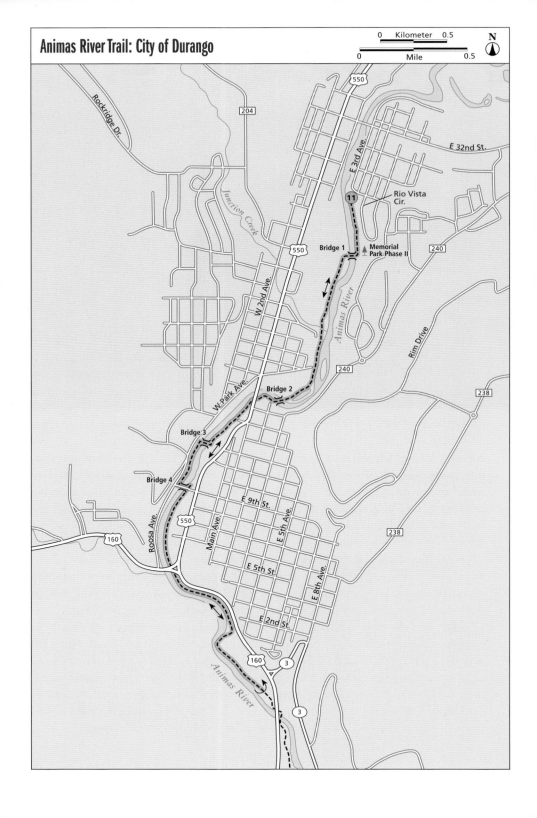

Bridge over Animas River on the Animas River Trail

and follow the trail south along the west side of the river to another bridge crossing at 2.0 miles. After turning left (east) to cross the bridge, the trail turns left (north) again and loops around and under the bridge you just crossed to continue south along the east side of the river. The trail narrows here for a bit and has some limited-visibility corners, so be careful. Cross under a bridge at 2.5 miles, pass the Durango dog park on you're right (west), and eventually arrive at one of Durango's proudest areas, the whitewater park. Pass by the whitewater park on your right (west) at 3.0 miles and continue on to Santa Rita Park. Arrive at Santa Rita Park, home to numerous outdoor activities and events in Durango, at 3.5 miles. The trail continues south from here, but for this description turn around here and return to the Memorial Park parking area and trailhead via the same route.

Miles and Directions

0.0 Begin hiking south on the paved trail from Memorial Park.

0.3 Cross a bridge and stay left (south) after crossing a set of railroad tracks.

0.7 Stay left (south) on the Animas River Trail.

1.2 Stay right (west) and hike through Rotary Park.

1.7 Cross a bridge and stay left (south).

2.0 Turn left (east) to cross over another bridge and then turn left (north) to circle around and under the bridge.

2.5 Travel under a bridge.

3.0 Pass by the whitewater park on the right (west).

3.5 Arrive at Santa Rita Park; then turn around and return via the same trail.

7.0 Arrive back at the parking area and trailhead.

12 Mancos State Park Trails

This series of trails that connect together to make a 4-mile loop through Mancos State Park make a great morning or afternoon hike. Mancos State Park is known more for the boating opportunities it offers, but many of the locals know how great the hiking and cross-country skiing can be as well. The network of trails even offers access to the Colorado Trail.

Start: Vista Trailhead and parking area
Distance: 4.0-mile loop
Hiking time: 2 to 2.5 hours
Difficulty: Moderate due to length
Trail surface: Forested trail
Best season: Spring and fall
Other trail users: Bikers and horseback riders
Canine compatibility: Leashed dogs permitted

Fees and permits: Day-use fees apply
Schedule: Open year-round
Maps: USGS: Rampart Hills, CO; trail map available at the day-use fee station
Trail contact: Mancos State Park, 1321 Railroad Ave., Dolores, CO 81323; (970) 882-2213; cpw.state.co.us/placestogo/parks/Mancos

---

Finding the trailhead: From Mancos, Colorado, drive north on South Main Street for 0.3 mile and then turn right (east) onto CR 42. Drive 4.2 miles on CR 42 and then turn left (west) onto CR N. Continue 0.4 mile to the park entrance and fee station. Turn right (north) after the fee station and park at the Vista Trailhead parking area. GPS: N37 24.056' / W108 16.160'

The Hike

Mancos State Park sits in an area surrounded by recreational opportunities. Not only does the park sit along the San Juan Skyway Scenic Byway, but just miles away to the west is Mesa Verde National Park and to the east is Durango. The San Juan Mountains surround the area, and not much farther west are Cortez and Dolores. The great thing about Mancos State Park is that it is home to many of the outdoor recreation activities that surround it. The park is home to the Jackson Gulch Reservoir, which is the water source for Mesa Verde and the Mancos Valley. Kayaking, canoeing, and limited motorized boating are all allowed on the 216 surface acres of water. The reservoir also provides great fishing, including yellow perch and rainbow trout. It is not uncommon to see ice fishing on the reservoir during the colder winter months. Snowshoeing and cross-country skiing tend to be popular activities in the wintertime, and when the snow melts, the horseback riders and hikers hit the trails.

The park offers thirty-two campsites in the campground, where there are no electric hookups but there are vault toilets and drinking water. One of the fun things about Mancos State Park is the two yurts that are available for rent. The yurts are heated in the wintertime and are available to rent year-round. There are about 5 miles of hiking trails located within the park, as well as access points to other trails outside

View of Mesa Verde National Park from Mancos State Park

the park. This description uses five different trails to create a 4-mile loop around the reservoir.

From the Vista Trailhead parking area, begin hiking north on the packed-dirt trail and quickly make a right (northeast) turn onto the Mule Deer Trail. Hike northeast along the reservoir as the trail descends into a somewhat boggy area that can be a little wet during certain seasons. Cross a small footbridge at 0.7 mile as the trail turns west. A sign here asks horseback riders to go around the bridge and allow for foot traffic only. After crossing the bridge continue hiking west into the northern campground, where there are toilets and a picnic area as well. Reach the Quarry Trailhead at 1.0 mile and continue hiking west from here on the Mountain Lion Trail. From here the trail begins a gradual climb up into ponderosa pine forest and moves away from the reservoir. After a short uphill the ground levels back out and you reach a trail junction at 1.5 miles.

Turn right (northeast) onto the Black Bear Trail to hike the longer portion of the loop. The Black Bear Trail also goes to the left (southwest), but this is the shorter route. Continue hiking northeast through the forest, and as the trail begins to turn left (west), you will pass an access trail to the national forest at 1.9 miles. The access trail continues northeast. Keep hiking west on the Black Bear Trail as views of Mesa

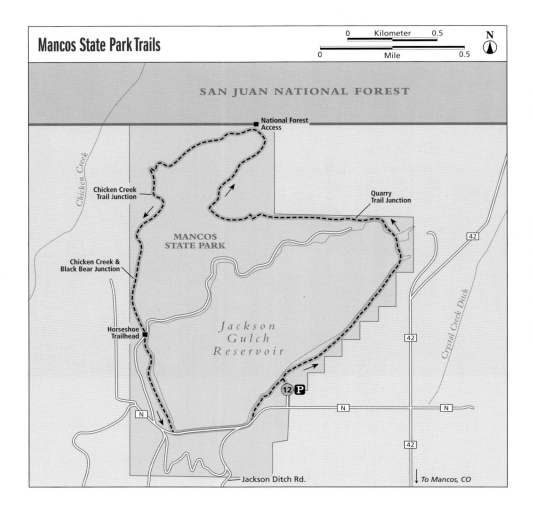

Mancos State Park Trails

SAN JUAN NATIONAL FOREST

National Forest
Access

Chicken Creek
Trail Junction

Quarry
Trail Junction

MANCOS
STATE PARK

Chicken Creek &
Black Bear Junction

Horseshoe
Trailhead

*Jackson
Gulch
Reservoir*

Chicken Creek

Crystal Creek Ditch

42

42

42

Jackson Ditch Rd.

To Mancos, CO

0   Kilometer   0.5

0   Mile   0.5

N

Verde National Park can be had just before descending into a valley and then eventually arriving at another trail junction at 2.5 miles. Turn left (south) to continue hiking on the Black Bear Trail toward the Chicken Creek Trailhead. Right (north) is the Chicken Creek Trail, which leads to the Colorado Trail.

Continuing south toward the Chicken Creek Trailhead, you'll pass the Black Bear Trail's southern loop access point on the left (east) at 2.9 miles. Continue south here and reach the Chicken Creek Trailhead at 3.0 miles. From the Chicken Creek Trailhead, continue hiking south onto the Horseshoe Trail. The Horseshoe Trail travels along the western edge of Jackson Gulch Reservoir and then turns left (east) at 3.5 miles to skirt the southern end of the reservoir. The trail here is very rocky and rugged. Arrive at the boat ramp at 3.8 miles and reconnect with the trail on the other side of the ramp as the trail turns northeast. At 4.0 miles turn right (south) to return to the Vista Trailhead and parking area.

Miles and Directions

0.0 From the Vista Trailhead and parking area, begin hiking north and quickly make a right (northeast) turn onto the Mule Deer Trail.

0.7 Come to and cross a small footbridge. Horseback riders are directed to go around.

1.0 Reach the junction with the Quarry Trailhead. Continue hiking west onto the Mountain Lion Trail.

1.5 Turn right (northeast) onto the Black Bear Trail.

1.9 The national forest access trail continues north. Turn left (west) to stay on the Black Bear Trail.

2.5 Turn left (south) to stay on the Black Bear/Chicken Creek Trails. The Chicken Creek Trail is to the right (north) and offers access to the Colorado Trail.

2.9 The southern loop portion of the Black Bear Trail joins from the left (east). Continue hiking south to the Chicken Creek Trailhead.

Trail junction

3.0 Come to the Chicken Creek Trailhead. Continue hiking south onto the Horseshoe Trail.

3.5 The trail curves to the left (east) and follows along the reservoir shoreline.

3.8 Reach the boat ramp and continue northeast on the Mule Deer Trail.

4.0 Come to the end of the loop and turn right (southeast) to return to the parking area and Vista Trailhead.

13 Prater Ridge Trail: Mesa Verde National Park

The Prater Ridge Trail in Mesa Verde National Park is a great half-day hike that offers something a little different from what you'd expect in the park. The park is known for its numerous ruins, but you won't find any on this hike. Instead, the trail climbs high and offers great views of the park and the surrounding area as it travels along Prater Ridge.

Start: Trailhead and parking area at the Morefield Campground
Distance: 7.4-mile lollipop
Hiking time: About 4 hours
Difficulty: Moderate due to length
Trail surface: Packed-dirt and rocky trail
Best season: Any
Other trail users: None
Canine compatibility: No dogs permitted

Fees and permits: Park entrance fee required
Schedule: Open year-round; check website for holiday closures
Maps: USGS: Moccasin Mesa, CO; trail map available at the visitor center
Trail contact: Mesa Verde National Park, PO Box 8, Mesa Verde, CO 81330; (970) 529-4465; www.nps.gov/meve/index.htm

Finding the trailhead: From Mancos, Colorado, drive 7.2 miles west on US 160 to the Mesa Verde National Park exit on the right (north). After exiting, turn left (south) onto CO 10 and drive 3.9 miles to the Morefield Campground. Turn right into the campground and drive 0.6 mile to the parking area and trailhead on the left (west). GPS: N37 17.808' / W108 25.097'

The Hike

President Theodore Roosevelt designated Mesa Verde National Park on June 29, 1906, in order to preserve the ancient works of man found in the park. What many visitors do not realize is that the park also contains a rich diversity of natural resources that alone are worthy of national park status. The park includes 8,500 acres of federally designated wilderness and is a Class I Airshed, the highest standard set by Congress under the Clean Air Act. In addition, Mesa Verde National Park covers just over 52,000 acres of the Colorado Plateau.

Mesa Verde is also unique in that it lies in the transition zone between the arid scrublands to the south and southwest and the forested high alpine environments of the Rocky Mountains to the north and northeast. Because of the park's unique geographic location, it is able to support four different plant communities. At the lowest elevation is the shrub-steppe community that includes the sagebrush valleys. As you gain elevation in the park, you will find the pinyon-juniper forests, and then the mountain shrub communities, and finally the Douglas firs and ponderosa pines. With all this diversity in climate and plant life, there is also a diverse wildlife population that includes resident and migratory mammals, birds, reptiles, amphibians, fishes, and

View of Sleeping Ute Mountain from Prater Ridge Trail

invertebrates. Deer, elk, and black bear can all be spotted in the park. Due to Mesa Verde's protected park status, many plant and animal species that are rarely seen in the region still exist in the park today, including breeding pairs of peregrine falcons and Mexican spotted owls. Many species of rare plants survive in protected parklands. Some of these rare plants, such as the Cliff Palace milkvetch, are found nowhere except in Mesa Verde.

The Prater Ridge Trail is a lot like the rich diversity of natural resources in the park that are overshadowed by all the ancient ruins of cliff dwellings. Many park visitors come to hike on trails that lead to ruins, but the Prater Ridge Trail does not offer any ruins; however, it does offer some of the best hiking and scenery in the park. Begin hiking northwest from the Prater Ridge Trail parking area and trailhead on the dirt trail. Come to a trail junction at 0.2 mile and stay left (northwest) on the Prater Ridge Trail. The trail to the right (north) is the Knife Edge Trail. Continue hiking uphill until you reach the top of the mesa at 0.8 mile. Turn right (northwest) at 1.1 miles to begin the loop portion of the hike.

The trail continues northwest, and hikers will soon start taking in beautiful views of the Montezuma Valley to the west, including a nice viewpoint at 2.4 miles where the Sleeping Ute Mountain is visible as well. From here the trail turns southeast and

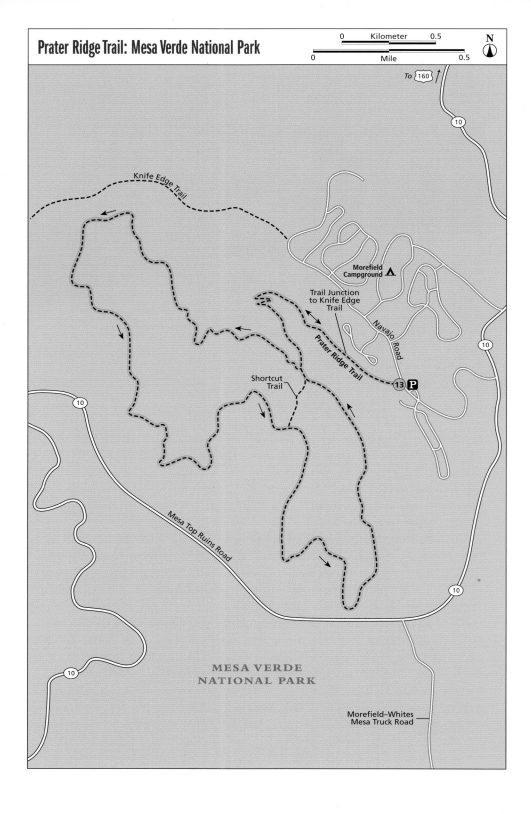

Prater Ridge Trail: Mesa Verde National Park

Kilometer
0 0.5

Mile
0 0.5

N

To 160

10

Knife Edge Trail

Morefield
Campground

Trail Junction
to Knife Edge
Trail

Navajo Road

Prater Ridge Trail

13 P

10

Shortcut
Trail

10

Mesa Top Ruins Road

10

10

MESA VERDE
NATIONAL PARK

Morefield–Whites
Mesa Truck Road

Trailhead

travels high above CO 10. Hikers can see far south through the park as they make their way along the rim of the mesa. At 4.3 miles you will reach a connector trail on the left (north) that presents an option for those looking to cut the hike short. Continue to the right (east) to hike the full loop. From here the trail loops south and then north along the mesa rim and eventually reaches the point where the connector trail you passed earlier connects again on the left (southwest) at 6.2 miles. Continue right (north) to 6.3 miles, where the loop portion of the hike ends, and turn right (north) to return to the trailhead and parking area at 7.4 miles.

Miles and Directions

0.0 Begin hiking northwest on the dirt trail as it climbs up the hill.

0.2 Stay left (northwest) on the Prater Ridge Trail. To the right (north) is the Knife Edge Trail.

0.8 Reach the end of the gradual ascent after a hairpin turn and switchbacks.

1.1 Turn right (northwest) to begin the loop portion of the hike.

2.4 Arrive at a good viewpoint for the Sleeping Ute Mountain and the Montezuma Valley to the west.

4.3 Reach a connector trail on the left (north). Continue to the right (east). (***Option:*** To cut the hike short, follow the connector trail for 0.3 mile and rejoin the main route at mile 6.2. This will reduce the overall hike distance to 5.7 miles.)

6.2 The connector trail joins from the left (southwest). Continue hiking to the right (north) to complete the loop.

6.3 Reach the end of the loop portion of the hike. Turn right (north) to return to the trailhead and parking area.

7.4 Arrive back at the start.

14 Petroglyph Point Trail: Mesa Verde National Park

The Petroglyph Point Trail in Mesa Verde National Park gives hikers a little bit of everything that the park has to offer. Hikers choosing this adventure will see some of the classic cliff dwellings that the park is known for, a beautiful petroglyph panel, and stunning views of the canyons and mesas in the park.

Start: Chapin Mesa Museum
Distance: 2.9-mile loop
Hiking time: 2 to 3 hours
Difficulty: Moderate due to rugged trail
Trail surface: Packed-dirt and rocky trail
Best season: Spring and fall
Other trail users: None
Canine compatibility: No dogs permitted

Fees and permits: Park entrance fee required
Schedule: Open year-round; check website for holiday closures
Maps: USGS: Moccasin Mesa, CO; trail map available at the visitor center
Trail contact: Mesa Verde National Park, PO Box 8, Mesa Verde, CO 81330; (970) 529-4465; www.nps.gov/meve/index.htm

Finding the trailhead: From Mancos, Colorado, drive 7.2 miles west on US 160 to the Mesa Verde National Park exit on the right (north). After exiting, turn left (south) onto CO 10, drive 20 miles to the stop sign, and turn right (west) toward the Spruce Tree House Ruins. Continue 0.8 mile to the parking area for the Chapin Mesa Museum and the Spruce Tree House Ruins. GPS: N37 11.057' / W108 29.306'

The Hike

Mesa Verde National Park is the largest archaeological preserve in the United States. Today the park protects nearly 5,000 known archaeological sites, 600 of which are cliff dwellings. The cliff dwellings of Mesa Verde are some of the most notable and best-preserved on the entire North American continent. It is believed that sometime around AD 1200, after living primarily on the mesa top for 600 years, many Ancestral Puebloans began building and living in pueblos beneath the overhanging cliffs and in caves. The structures here range in size from one-room storage units to villages of more than 150 rooms. Cliff Palace, located in the park, is believed to be the largest cliff dwelling ruin in North America. The inhabitants of the dwellings continued to farm the mesa tops as they resided in the alcoves, repairing, remodeling, and constructing new rooms for nearly a century. Researchers say that by the late 1270s, the people in this area began migrating south into present-day New Mexico and Arizona. By 1300 the Ancestral Puebloan occupation of Mesa Verde ended, and all that remains are the ancient ruins.

Some of the most notable and famous ruins within the park include the Balcony House, Cliff Palace, Long House, Mug House, Oak Tree House, Square Tower House, and the ruin visited in this hike description: Spruce Tree House. Many of these larger

Spruce Tree House Ruins

cliff dwellings require a park ranger tour guide for up-close views. The Spruce Tree House, however, is open year-round (except for weather closures and holiday closures) and allows visitors to hike down to the ruins on their own. A park ranger or two are at the ruins during operating hours to answer questions. The Spruce Tree House is the third-largest village in the park and is believed to have been home to around sixty or eighty people. The dwelling has 130 rooms and 8 kivas, including a reconstructed kiva that visitors are allowed to climb down into if they so choose.

To begin your hike to the Spruce Tree House and then to Pictograph Point, begin hiking on the paved trail at the southeast corner of the Chapin Mesa Museum. Just a few feet down the trail you will see your return trail on the left (north). Continue to the right (east) on the paved trail as it begins descending into Spruce Canyon. At 0.2 mile you will reach a trail junction. Stay left (north) to visit the Spruce Tree House Ruins. Heading right (northeast) will skip the ruins and lead to the Petroglyph Point and Spruce Canyon Trails. The trail continues north up into the canyon and passes a spring before turning south and arriving at the ruins at 0.3 mile. After your visit to the Spruce Tree House, continue hiking south past the ruins and drop down farther into Spruce Canyon. At 0.4 mile turn left (south) toward the Petroglyph Point and Spruce Canyon Trails. Turn left (east) again at 0.5 mile onto the Petroglyph Point Trail.

Continue hiking up the rock stairs as the Petroglyph Point Trail makes its way to about the midpoint of the canyon wall on the east side of Spruce Canyon. The canyon is littered with Utah juniper, Douglas fir, Gambel oak, and pine. The trail continues

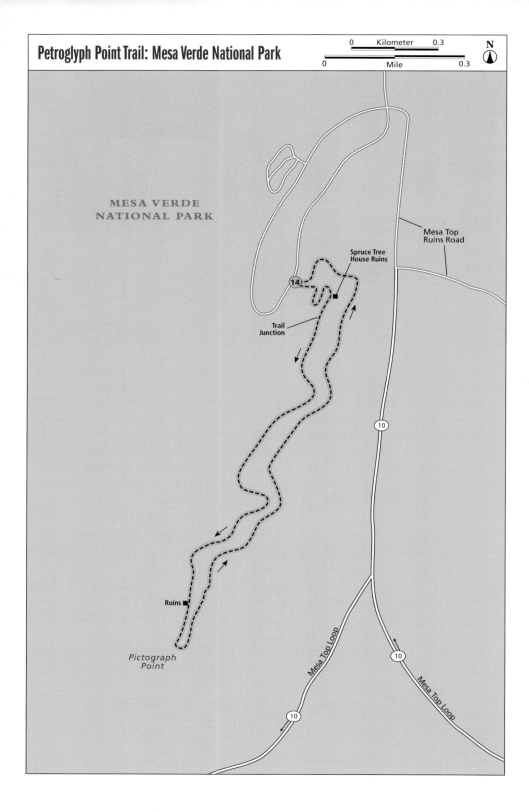

Petroglyph Point Trail: Mesa Verde National Park

0   Kilometer   0.3

0   Mile   0.3

N

MESA VERDE
NATIONAL PARK

Mesa Top
Ruins Road

Spruce Tree
House Ruins

14

Trail
Junction

10

Ruins ■

Pictograph
Point

Mesa Top Loop

10

Mesa Top Loop

10

to twist and turn along the canyon wall and even includes a tight squeeze through a couple of boulders and a lot of short ups and downs. Come to a small ruin up in an alcove on the left (east) at 1.2 miles, probably a storage place at one time. Not far from here you will arrive at Pictograph Point at 1.5 miles. Pictograph Point is the largest known collection of petroglyphs in the park. A trail guide can be purchased at the beginning of the trail or in the visitor center to help you interpret the symbols.

From Pictograph Point the trail continues south for just a short distance as it climbs up the mesa top and turns northeast. Once at the top, follow the trail as it skirts along the canyon rim and offers great views of the canyon below. At 2.3 miles you can get a great view of the canyon as it stretches to the southwest as well as a view of the museum to the northwest. At 2.7 miles the trail leaves pinyon pine and Utah juniper shrubland and turns west to cross over a slickrock section where you are able to see the Spruce Tree House Ruins down below to the southeast. After crossing the slickrock and snapping a few last photos of the ruins, you will return to the paved section of trail. Turn right (west) and return to the trailhead, museum, and parking area at 2.9 miles.

Petroglyphs along the trail

▶ **What's the difference between a petroglyph and a pictograph? Both terms refer to rock art produced by Native Americans in the past. Petroglyphs are pictures or symbols that have been carved into the rock. Pictographs are painted onto the rock surface.**

Miles and Directions

0.0 Start hiking east on the paved trail from the southeast corner of the Chapin Mesa Museum. You soon pass the dirt and rock return trail on the left (north); stay right on the paved trail toward the Spruce Tree House Ruins.

0.2 Stay left (north) to visit the ruins; the trail to the right (east) bypasses the ruins.

0.3 Come to the Spruce Tree House Ruins. Continue hiking south.

0.4 Turn left (south) onto the Petroglyph Point and Spruce Canyon Trails.

0.5 Turn left (east) up the stairs onto the Petroglyph Point Trail.

1.2 Reach a small set of ruins in the cliff side.

1.5 Arrive at Pictograph Point. The trail climbs to the top of the mesa and turns left (northeast).

2.3 Enjoy nice views of the canyon to the southwest and of the museum to the northwest.

2.7 Cross a slickrock area and see Spruce Tree House Ruins down below.

2.9 Turn right (west) back onto the paved trail and return to the Chapin Mesa Museum.

Honorable Mentions

F Spruce Canyon Trail: Mesa Verde National Park

This 2.4-mile loop trail is located at the southern end of Mesa Verde National Park. It drops down into Spruce Canyon and allows hikers an opportunity to explore a canyon floor in the park. It is a popular trail for hiking but rarely feels crowded. Rugged and hilly at each end, the trail crosses through a canyon and lets hikers experience the plants and wildlife that live in this challenging habitat. To get to the trailhead from Mancos, Colorado, drive 7.2 miles west on US 160 to the Mesa Verde National Park exit on the right (north). After exiting, turn left (south) onto CO 10, drive 20 miles to the stop sign, and turn right (west) toward the Spruce Tree House Ruins. Continue 0.8 mile to the parking area for the Chapin Mesa Museum and the Spruce Tree House Ruins. Locate the trailhead at the southern end of the Chapin Mesa Museum. For more information on the Spruce Canyon Trail, contact Mesa Verde National Park, PO Box 8, Mesa Verde, CO 81330; (970) 529-4465; www.nps.gov/meve/index.htm.

G Rock Creek Trail: Canyons of the Ancients National Monument

Located in the Canyons of the Ancients National Monument, the Rock Creek Trail is a loop hike that is a multiuse trail. Many mountain bikers come to the area for riding. The Canyons of the Ancients is filled with Ancestral Puebloan archaeological sites. Please respect the ancient ruins when visiting the area so that the site will stay open to the public and many more people can come and enjoy the rich history here. To find the trailhead from Cortez, Colorado, drive 12.1 miles on CR G to the Sand Canyon South Trailhead and parking area on the right (north) side of the road. The Sand Canyon and Rock Creek Trails share the same trailhead. For more information on the area, contact Canyons of the Ancients National Monument and Anasazi Heritage Center, 27501 CO 184, Dolores, CO 81323; (970) 882-5600; www.blm.gov/co/st/en/nm/canm.html.

H West Mancos / Transfer Trails: San Juan National Forest

Located near Mancos, Colorado, the Transfer Recreation Area provides access to a network of hiking trails in southwestern Colorado. Hikers can choose from a variety of trail connections to make shorter or longer hikes depending on time or ability. The Big Al Trail offers interpretive signs and bench seating along the way, while the West Mancos Trail and Transfer Trail offer a more challenging trek down to the Mancos River Canyon and back up. To reach the trailhead from Mancos, drive 0.3 mile north on CO 184 and then turn right (east) onto CR 42. Continue 10.2 miles on CR 42 to the Transfer Campground and trailhead parking on the left (west). Locate the trailhead across the road (east). For more information contact San Juan National Forest Service, 15 Burnett Ct., Durango, CO 81301; (970) 247-4874; www.fs.usda.gov/activity/sanjuan/recreation/hiking.

Sharkstooth Trail: San Juan National Forest

Located north of Mancos, Colorado, the Sharkstooth Trail is another starting point that offers several hiking options for hikers looking for an adventure. Hikers leaving the Sharkstooth Trail also have options to continue hiking on trails like the Colorado Trail and the Highline National Recreation Trail as well as access to several other trails along the way. Sharkstooth, Centennial, and Hesperus Mountains are all peaks that can be reached from this trailhead as well. To reach the trailhead from Mancos, drive 0.3 mile north on CO 184 and then turn right (east) onto CR 42. Continue 12 miles on CR 42 to FR 350 and turn right; then continue 7.8 miles to the Sharkstooth Trail trailhead. For more information contact San Juan National Forest Service, 15 Burnett Ct., Durango, CO 81301; (970) 247-4874; www.fs.usda.gov/activity/sanjuan/recreation/hiking.

J Crater Lake Trail: San Juan National Forest

Located at the base of Twilight Peak and providing access to Snowdon Peak, the hike to Crater Lake is an excellent long day hike or can be done as an enjoyable overnight trip. The 11-mile out-and-back trip is a great high-altitude hike that begins at around 10,700 feet and tops out at around 11,700 feet. Hikers will experience the beauty of an alpine lake, Crater Lake, as well as the jagged and rugged San Juan Mountains that surround. From Durango, Colorado, drive about 45 miles north on US 550. Turn right (east) into the signed Andrews Lake picnic area. Continue 0.5 mile to the parking area and trailheads. For more information contact San Juan National Forest Service, 15 Burnett Ct., Durango, CO 81301; (970) 247-4874; www.fs.usda.gov/activity/sanjuan/recreation/hiking.

K Highland Mary Lakes Trail: San Juan National Forest

Located near Silverton, Colorado, and in the Weminuche Wilderness, this 4-mile round-trip hike is an alpine lake lover's dream. Hikers looking for a longer trip can continue past Highland Mary Lakes and hike to the Verde Lakes and even on to the Continental Divide Trail if so desired. Popular with both hikers and horseback riders, the trail offers great access to alpine lakes and stunning views of the Grenadier Mountain Range. To reach the trailhead, drive 46 miles north on US 550 from Durango, Colorado, to the tiny mountain town of Silverton; then drive east on CR 2 for 4.1 miles. Turn right (south) onto CR 4 and drive 4.6 miles to the trailhead and parking area. For more information contact San Juan National Forest Service, 15 Burnett Ct., Durango, CO 81301; (970) 247-4874; www.fs.usda.gov/activity/sanjuan/recreation/hiking.

New Mexico Region

Welcome to the Land of Enchantment! The northwestern New Mexico portion of the Four Corners region is a vast and magnificent area filled with mystery, unusual rock formations, high plains, desert plants and wildlife, and spectacular blue skies. Much of the land is Navajo reservation. The largest city in the Four Corners is here in New Mexico. Farmington has a population of nearly 50,000 people and offers the largest variety of shopping in the area. It's a great place to begin your Four Corners adventure. The city itself offers hiking, mountain biking, boating, and fishing right within the city limits. The area has also become a recent attraction for the film industry, having played host to several full-length films and television episodes.

The highlights of the New Mexico region include mesmerizing rock formations, wind-carved badlands, a dry and arid climate, ancient ruins, and a small collection of natural arches that have been carved out of this rugged and challenging landscape over many, many years. Thirteen of the trails in this book are found scattered throughout this mysterious area. In 2013 New Mexico announced more than 1.5 million national park visits that resulted in over $81 million in economic benefit for the state from its thirteen National Park Service–managed lands. Only two of those national parks are included in this guide, but they offer some of the most spectacular ruins in the region. Chaco Culture National Historical Park and Aztec Ruins National Monument are located here. A trip to Chaco Culture National Historical Park will have visitors wondering to themselves, "How did they do that?" and Aztec Ruins National Monument proudly boasts the largest reconstructed great kiva in the United States. Kivas are rooms that were built underground by the Pueblo people, typically for religious and communal purposes.

The other trails found in the New Mexico region are located on Bureau of Land Management land and in the city of Farmington. Many of the trails and attractions in the New Mexico region in this guide tend to be not well-known areas and/or hikes. Developments like trailhead signs may be few or even nonexistent at some of the locations. However, if you enjoy having great trails mostly to yourself, the lack of development won't be an issue at all, as you may find yourself to be the only one on the trail. That being said, use caution in some areas, as even the trails are undeveloped and you will need to have a good sense of direction and be familiar with a map and compass. Hiking here has many opportunities and looks to be getting better!

◀ *Penasco Blanco Ruins (hike 21)*

15 Dancing Horse Trail: Four Corners Monument

It doesn't seem right to not include a hike at the Four Corners Monument in a guide to hiking the Four Corners, so here it is. The 1.5-mile round-trip Dancing Horse Trail at the Four Corners Monument offers a short and fairly easy hike in New Mexico and Colorado to a mesa that offers great views of the San Juan River as well as the surrounding area.

Start: Four Corners Monument parking area
Distance: 1.5-mile out-and-back
Hiking time: 1 to 2 hours
Difficulty: Moderate due to rocky terrain
Trail surface: Dirt trail and rocky path
Best season: Spring and fall
Other trail users: Horseback riders
Canine compatibility: Leashed dogs permitted

Fees and permits: Fee required to enter the monument
Schedule: Open year-round
Maps: USGS: Teec Nos Pos, AZ-CO-NM-UT
Trail contact: Navajo Nation Parks and Recreation, Building 36A, AZ 264 East at Indian Route 12, Window Rock, AZ 86515; (928) 871-6647; www.navajonationparks.org/htm/fourcorners.htm

Finding the trailhead: From Teec Nos Pos, Arizona, drive north on US 160 for 5.6 miles. Turn left (northwest) onto NM 597/Four Corners Road and drive 0.4 mile to the parking area. GPS: N36 59.935'/W109 2.710'

The Hike

What would a guide to the Four Corners be without a hike at the actual Four Corners Monument? The Four Corners Monument marks the quadripoint in the southwestern United States, and the only place in the United States where four states meet at such a point, where the states of Arizona, Colorado, New Mexico, and Utah meet. The monument also marks the boundary between two Native American governments, the Navajo Nation reservation and the Ute Mountain Tribe reservation.

The monument is maintained by the Navajo Nation Parks and Recreation Department and consists of a large area that has been finished with very nice stonework and then surrounded by a set of vendor stands. During peak tourist season these stands will be filled with local Navajo and Ute artists displaying their art for sale and other vendors selling souvenirs and food. A debate that started many years ago about whether the monument is in the correct location still lingers today. Many people say that the boundary lines are off, and more than likely, with the technology used back in the day to determine these lines, this is probably true. Those that are really nitpicky about the exact point can probably search for and discover the right location, but your photo won't be quite as nice as the ones being taken at the monument.

Visitors at the Four Corners Monument

The monument does require a fee to enter and does have a few amenities. In addition to the vendors, there is a large RV parking and picnic area as well as a couple of restrooms sitting in the New Mexico quadrant. This is also the location of the Dancing Horse Trailhead. We started the hike for this description from the actual monument, though. From the Four Corners Monument, begin hiking south and then east through the parking and picnic area. At the eastern end of the picnic area is a sign for the Dancing Horse Trail at 0.2 mile. Follow the trail as it turns southeast and heads directly for a mesa that stretches across the New Mexico and Colorado border. The area looks almost volcanic with all the dark rocks lying around. You'll reach a small saddle at 0.3 mile while still in New Mexico where the trail system offers a few options. Turn right (southwest) to take in the views at the Short Hair and San Juan River overlooks at 0.4 mile before backtracking to the main trail to continue your hike.

Turn right (northeast) back onto the main trail and continue hiking gradually uphill along the ridge of the mesa. Pass the Slowman Point on the left (northwest) at 0.6 mile as the trail gets a bit steeper and the footing becomes a bit more uncertain. As you reach the top of the mesa, you will cross over into Colorado and continue hiking northeast until the mesa ends at 0.8 mile. Turn around here and return to the parking area and monument at 1.5 miles.

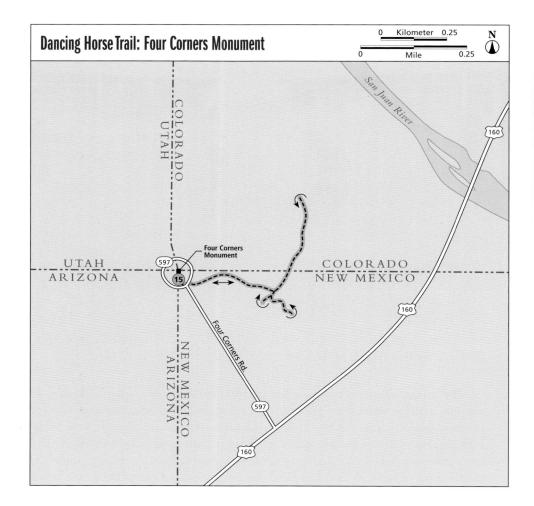

Dancing Horse Trail: Four Corners Monument

Miles and Directions

0.0 Start at the Four Corners Monument and begin hiking south and then east through the picnic area.

0.2 At the east end of the picnic area, pick up the trail and continue hiking east.

0.3 Come to a saddle and turn right (south) to visit the Short Hair and San Juan River overlooks.

0.4 Reach the San Juan River overlook.

0.5 Return to the main trail and turn right (northeast).

0.6 Pass the Slowman Point on the left (northwest).

0.8 The trail ends at the end of the mesa. Return to the parking area via the same route.

1.5 Arrive back at the parking area.

16 Anasazi Arch Trail: Bureau of Land Management

New Mexico is not as well-known for its arches as nearby Utah. However, arches like Anasazi Arch are nothing to shrug your shoulders at. The very short hike to the arch requires a drive out into the New Mexico oil fields, some rock scrambling, and even a little route finding. What seems like a short and sweet hike requires a little effort that is well worth it. Hikers with an adventurous spirit can explore for hours after locating the arch.

Start: Parking area
Distance: 0.5-mile out-and-back
Hiking time: 1 to 2 hours
Difficulty: Moderate due to rock scramble
Trail surface: Dirt and sand trail
Best season: Any
Other trail users: Horseback riders
Canine compatibility: Leashed dogs permitted

Fees and permits: No fees or permits required
Schedule: Open year-round
Maps: USGS: Cedar Hill, NM
Trail contact: Bureau of Land Management, 6251 College Blvd., Ste. A, Farmington, NM 87402; (505) 564-7600; www.blm.gov/nm/st/en/fo/Farmington_Field_Office.html

Finding the trailhead: From Aztec, New Mexico, drive north on US 550 for 10.8 miles. Turn left (west) onto CR 2300 and drive 1.3 miles. Stay right at the Y intersection onto CR 2310. Drive 2.8 miles on CR 2310 and turn right onto the unsigned road just past a series of oil and gas plants. Drive 0.2 mile on the dirt road while keeping to the left (gas and oil plants on the right) to the parking area. GPS: N36 59.764' / W107 54.627'

The Hike

Northwestern New Mexico is a place that offers a wealth of natural and cultural history. This remote and rarely visited landscape may not be on the radar of many outdoor enthusiasts, but it should be. Sites like Chaco Culture National Historical Park, Aztec Ruins National Monument, and Salmon Ruins offer a glimpse into the lives of the Ancestral Puebloans, the people who called this region home nearly 1,000 years ago. The frigid waters of the San Juan River offer some of the best fly fishing in the country. The few mountain bike trails, such as the Alien Run Trail, are fun and fast. Hikers willing to explore areas that are off-trail will find a vast array of hiking opportunities.

One sight that you will not want to miss is the Anasazi Arch, also referred to as the Cox Canyon Arch. This natural arch is located north of Aztec, New Mexico, near the Colorado/New Mexico state line. A rough "trail" leads the way to this beautiful sandstone arch. Visitors should be capable of basic route-finding skills and be ready and willing to do a little rock scrambling in order to reach the arch. The arch itself is a lovely and delicate shape, slightly wider than it is tall. Particularly stunning at

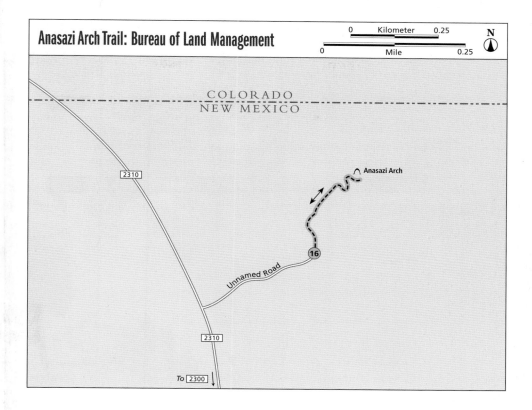

Anasazi Arch Trail: Bureau of Land Management

COLORADO
NEW MEXICO

2310

Anasazi Arch

16

Unnamed Road

2310

To 2300

sunset and sunrise, the nearly 40-foot-tall arch is a worthy destination in and of itself, although most will find it nearly impossible to not explore the trail-less landscape that surrounds it.

From the small, unsigned parking area, begin hiking north into the rocky wash. There is a large, prominent rock spire near the trailhead and parking area that you might use as a landmark to confirm that you are indeed in the right canyon.

Follow the well-worn but unmarked footpath that skirts along the northern edge of this small box canyon. The arch is not visible at the trailhead, but after a very short distance, it will come into view on the northeast horizon. There are three areas that require hand-and-foot-style rock scrambling. While you will not need ropes or specialized climbing equipment, we recommend hiking this trail with a partner, particularly if you have not hiked this area before.

The first small cliff you will encounter is approximately 5 feet tall. Look for good hand- and footholds and, if possible, have your hiking companion spot you. Continue northeast, hiking up-canyon. After a very short distance, you will again need to do

Anasazi Arch

some hand-and-foot-style rock scrambling. Less confident climbers will be happy to have a companion to spot their moves in this section. The first section is an easy scramble of about 4 feet onto a small ledge that leads to the top of the cliff. The next scramble is also about 4 feet. This one is more exposed, but has several chiseled hand-and footholds to help you along the way. Remember, you will have to climb down this section on your return trip.

Once out of the wash, hike northeast a short distance to the arch. Keen eyes may spot several rock cairns or footprints of previous visitors along the way. Come to the Anasazi Arch at 0.25 mile. Some will find this a perfect destination. Others will be compelled to explore further the large rock shelf where the arch is located before returning to the parking area via the same route. Rumor has it that there is another arch or two on this shelf!

Miles and Directions

0.0 Begin hiking north into the wash to the left of the large rock spire.

0.1 Follow the well-worn footpath up and out of the box canyon into another wash. A bit of rock scrambling is required.

0.2 Hike up and out of the wash to the right (northeast).

0.25 Arrive at Anasazi Arch. Return to the trailhead and parking area via the same route.

0.5 Arrive back at the parking area.

◀ *Rock spire near the beginning of the trail*

17 Simon Canyon Ruin Trail: Bureau of Land Management

For the best views hike the Simon Canyon Ruin Trail during prime fall foliage season. Don't be fooled, though; this 1.8-mile out-and-back hike offers some great views year-round. Hikers who make their way to the Simon Canyon Ruin will not only get great views of the canyon and ruin, but they may also catch glimpses of birds of prey that circle the canyon in this area.

Start: Simon Canyon trailhead and parking area
Distance: 1.8-mile out-and-back
Hiking time: 1 to 2 hours
Difficulty: Easy
Trail surface: Rock and dirt trail
Best season: Spring and fall
Other trail users: None

Canine compatibility: Leashed dogs permitted
Fees and permits: No fees or permits required
Schedule: Open year-round
Maps: USGS: Archuleta, NM
Trail contact: Bureau of Land Management, 6251 College Blvd., Ste. A, Farmington, NM 87402; (505) 564-7600; www.blm.gov/nm/st/en/fo/Farmington_Field_Office.html

Finding the trailhead: From Aztec, New Mexico, drive east on NM 173 for 17.3 miles to CR 4280. Turn left (north) onto CR 4280 and drive 3.1 miles to the Simon Canyon parking area and trailhead. GPS: N36 49.403'/W107 39.618'

The Hike

The Simon Canyon Ruin Trail is located in the Simon Canyon Area of Critical Environmental Concern and is near Navajo Lake State Park. The area is about 3,900 acres in size and allows a few forms of recreation including fishing, hiking, and backpacking. The parking area and trailhead is nicely developed with plenty of parking space, a vault toilet, and a picnic area. There is also access to the San Juan River Trail from this point. The quality waters of the San Juan River, located very nearby, attract fishing enthusiasts from all over the United States. Several full-service guiding companies are located along the river and in some cases also offer lodging. The river flows right by the mouth of Simon Canyon, where the trailhead is located.

This sandstone canyon has steep to very steep as well as rough and broken terrain. The landscape here consists of shrubs, cacti, cottonwood trees found near the water source running through the canyon, pinyon and juniper trees, and even some ponderosa pine up on the higher sections of the canyon rim. The diverse canyon landscape provides habitat for a variety of bird and mammal species as well. Wildlife such as golden eagle, prairie falcon, great horned owl, porcupine, beaver, and deer can all be spotted in or

Simon Canyon Ruin ▶

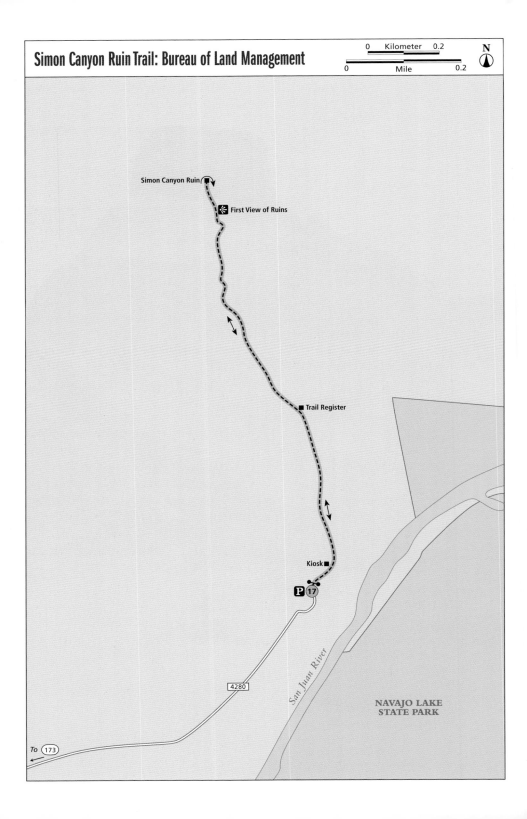

Simon Canyon Ruin Trail: Bureau of Land Management

0   Kilometer   0.2

0   Mile   0.2

N

Simon Canyon Ruin

First View of Ruins

Trail Register

Kiosk

P 17

4280

San Juan River

NAVAJO LAKE
STATE PARK

To 173

above the canyon. Because of all that the canyon provides, humans have been able to live in the area as well. Simon Canyon Ruin is a Navajo *pueblito* and sits up high on the eastern side of the canyon overlooking the canyon drainage. The ruin dates back to 1754 and is unique because it sits so far north of the San Juan River, which is considered to be the border between

Simon Canyon

the Navajo and the Utes. The ruin is a one-room structure built and perched on top of a large boulder. The inhabitants had notched hand- and footholds high up on the boulder and used a log to reach the holds from the ground. A rope was tied to the log so they could pull the log up when enemies were around.

From the Simon Canyon parking area and trailhead, begin hiking northeast through the gate that keeps vehicles from driving into the wash. Once in the wash at 0.1 mile, you will come to the Navajo Lake State Park and San Juan River Trail sign. Turn left (north) here to begin hiking up the right (east) side of the wash where the footpath becomes more evident. The trail leaves the wash to the right (east) and travels up a two-wheel-drive road and passes an oil and gas rigging station. Just past the station at 0.3 mile is the trailhead register and a sign that indicates "Foot Trail." From here the trail follows along the rim of the canyon on the east side. There are numerous places to walk to the edge of the canyon and look for wildlife or just enjoy the scenery. In the fall the cottonwoods provide a spectacular fall foliage show. After a short hike you will arrive at the Simon Canyon Ruin at 0.9 mile. A small interpretive sign has been placed near the ruin. Please respect the area and do not attempt to climb the boulder and reach the ruin. Turn around here and return to the trailhead and parking area via the same route at 1.8 miles.

Miles and Directions

0.0 Begin hiking northeast through the gate at the north end of the parking area.

0.1 After hiking down into a wash, you will come to a Navajo Lake State Park and San Juan River Trail sign. Turn left (north) to hike up onto the east rim of Simon Canyon.

0.3 Come to a foot trail sign and trail register.

0.9 Arrive at the Simon Canyon Ruin. Return to the trailhead and parking area via the same route.

1.8 Arrive back at the parking area.

18 Alien Run Trail: Bureau of Land Management

The highlight of this hike is the supposed alien UFO crash landing site. Hikers will enjoy a beautiful walk along the northern rim of Hart Canyon on their way to the crash site and then make their way across the high plains desert landscape on the return portion of the loop. Be sure to obey the directional travel rules that apply to the trail as it is primarily a mountain biking trail. The counterclockwise travel directions apply to all hikers and bikers.

Start: Alien Run parking area and trailhead
Distance: 8.6-mile loop
Hiking time: 4 to 5 hours
Difficulty: Moderate due to length
Trail surface: Slickrock, dirt trail, and road crossings
Best season: Late spring and fall
Other trail users: Bikers

Canine compatibility: Leashed dogs permitted
Fees and permits: No fees or permits required
Schedule: Open year-round
Maps: USGS: Spring Lake, NM
Trail contact: Bureau of Land Management, 6251 College Blvd., Ste. A, Farmington, NM 87402; (505) 564-7600; www.blm.gov/nm/st/en/fo/Farmington_Field_Office.html

Finding the trailhead: From Aztec, New Mexico, drive about 4 miles north on US 550 and turn right (east) onto CR 2770. Drive 2.8 miles on CR 2770 and turn left (north) onto the unsigned oil field road. Continue 0.5 mile north, cross a cattle guard, and turn right (east) onto another unsigned road. Drive 0.5 mile until the road dead-ends at the Alien Run Trail parking area and trailhead. GPS: N36 52.663'/W107 53.515'

The Hike

Here you go, *X-Files* fans. The story goes like this. In early March of 1948, an unidentified aircraft was spotted near Los Alamos, New Mexico, over the National Laboratory. Two weeks later, on March 25, there were reports of a similar-looking aircraft landing in or near Hart Canyon just north of Aztec, New Mexico. Witnesses say the aircraft had been shot at by the United States military and that the Los Alamos Radar Station tracked the controlled landing to this point. The Air Force and the Army coordinated a recovery operation that took 2 weeks to remove a 99.99-foot-diameter spacecraft from the canyon rim. At 18 feet tall, the craft is said to be the largest and most intact UFO to have been recovered. In addition to the craft, as many as sixteen charred bodies were recovered as well.

Locals believe that the United States military covered up the entire crash and all the events leading up to it and after it. It is said that the craft and the bodies were taken to Wright-Patterson Air Force Base in Dayton, Ohio. The crash, cover-up, and numerous other incidents were discussed every year at the Aztec UFO Symposium from 1997 until its end in 2011.

Alleged UFO crash site along the trail

Sagebrush and slickrock along Alien Run Trail

To visit the alien crash site near Aztec, and to find out if "the truth is out there," you'll need to make your way to the Alien Run Trail at Hart Canyon. The Alien Run Trail actually began as a mountain biking trail that was built as a possible fund-raising opportunity for the Aztec UFO Symposium in 1999. A local Aztec family built the trail system on Bureau of Land Management property. The trail has continued to be improved over the years, and the BLM has graciously opened its doors to foot traffic as well. Motorized vehicles and horses are not allowed on the trail.

From the Alien Run Trail parking area and trailhead, begin hiking east, following the directional arrows that point in a counterclockwise direction. This is a one-way trail. Please obey the trail rules and regulations. The trail travels along the northern rim of Hart Canyon for almost the entire first half of the hike. At 0.6 mile look down into the canyon to the south and check out all the unique rock formations along the canyon wall. Continue hiking east along the rim and reach some private property signs at 1.6 miles. There are a few places where the trail borders private property; please respect the landowner's request to stay off the private land. At 2.1 miles you'll cross a section of slickrock and at 2.3 miles reach a sign directing riders and hikers to the Black Hole. Stay left (east) to continue on the main trail. The Black Hole is a slickrock area where bikers go to ride and pull off tricks.

Alien Run Trail: Bureau of Land Management

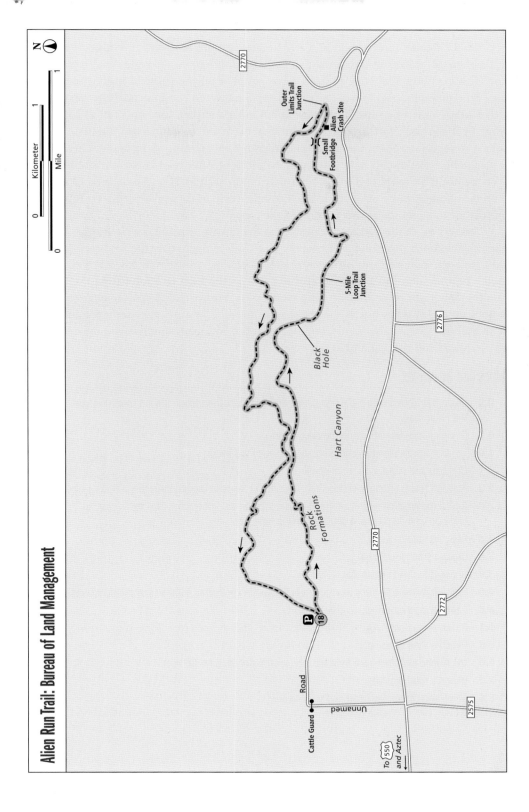

N

0   Kilometer   1

0   Mile   1

2770

Outer Limits Trail Junction

Alien Crash Site

Small Footbridge

5-Mile Loop Trail Junction

Black Hole

Hart Canyon

Rock Formations

2776

P

18

Road

Unnamed

Cattle Guard

2770

2772

2575

To 550 and Aztec

You'll come to another trail sign at 2.6 miles that directs riders and hikers north if they are just riding or hiking the 5-mile loop. Continue to the right (east) toward the alien crash site. The New Mexico desert is full of oil and gas field roads, and this area is no different; cross one of these roads at 3.5 miles and continue northeast on the other side. Come to a small footbridge at 3.8 miles and then hike up a hill to begin your final approach to the crash site. You'll arrive at the crash site at 3.9 miles. The area is strangely devoid of the shrubs and trees that are growing all around it. There is a plaque here that discusses the history of the incident. After your visit to the site, hike east for just a bit more to a trail junction. A newer section of trail called the Outer Limits continues east from here at the 4.0-mile mark. Make a sharp left turn to the northwest to begin the return portion of the loop.

This section of the trail moves away from the canyon rim and travels through the high plains desert shrubland. Pinyon pine and Utah juniper cover the landscape. You will cross a few more roads on the way back, including crossings at 4.8, 5.1, and 5.8 miles. Not far after the third road crossing, the 5-mile loop trail joins from the left (south). Stay right to continue hiking west on the return trail. A final road crossing comes up at 7.2 miles just as the trail begins heading in a northwesterly direction. The trail then approaches a private property fence and turns southwest to return to the trailhead and parking area at 8.6 miles.

Miles and Directions

0.0 Begin hiking east from the parking area and trailhead. The trail on the left (north) will be the return trail.

0.6 See cool rock formations on the right (south).

1.6 The trail travels along private property fencing to the south.

2.1 Come to and cross a slickrock opening.

2.3 Stay left (east) on the Alien Run Trail. The path to the right (south) goes to the Black Hole.

2.6 Reach the junction for the shorter 5-mile option on the left (north). Stay right (east) to cross an oil field road and continue on the long loop.

3.5 Reach a road crossing.

3.8 Cross a small footbridge.

3.9 Arrive at the alien crash site.

4.0 Stay left as the trail turns west to return. The Outer Limits Trail continues to the right (east).

4.8 Reach a road crossing.

5.1 Reach a road crossing.

5.8 Reach a road crossing.

6.0 The 5-mile loop trail joins from the left (south). Continue hiking west.

7.2 Reach a road crossing.

8.6 Arrive back at the trailhead and parking area.

19 Angel Peak Trail: Bureau of Land Management

Discover the mystery of the Angel Peak Scenic Area and the Four Corners' version of the badlands. The beauty of the landscape will amaze hikers visiting this magical area. This 1.6-mile out-and-back hike takes hikers along a narrow ridge and out into badlands for amazing views of Angel Peak. Photographers should consider an evening/sunset hike to capture the perfect picture.

Start: Gate at the northeast corner of the pavilion
Distance: 1.6-mile out-and-back
Hiking time: 1 to 2 hours
Difficulty: Easy
Trail surface: Dirt path
Best season: Spring and fall
Other trail users: None

Canine compatibility: Leashed dogs permitted
Fees and permits: No fees or permits required
Schedule: Open year-round
Maps: USGS: Huerfanito Peak, NM
Trail contact: Bureau of Land Management, 6251 College Blvd., Ste. A, Farmington, NM 87402; (505) 564-7600; www.blm.gov/nm/st/en/fo/Farmington_Field_Office.html

Finding the trailhead: From Bloomfield, New Mexico, drive south on US 550 for about 15 miles to CR 7175. Turn left (east) onto CR 7175 and drive 6.2 miles to the pavilion located at the eastern part of the scenic area and campground. GPS: N36 32.919' / W107 51.597'

The Hike

Managed by the Bureau of Land Management, Angel Peak Scenic Area is approximately 10,000 acres of rough and rugged desert landscape ripe for exploration. Hikers and photographers alike will find this little-known area quite exciting. While there are very limited established trails, there are plenty of hiking options along the canyon rim.

Located near Bloomfield, New Mexico, and rising up nearly 7,000 feet, Angel Peak is considered a landmark in the area. The monolith can be seen from quite a distance in any direction. While the peak itself is quite impressive, the surrounding badlands are equally scenic. Bands of yellow, gray, and maroon sandstone, siltstone, and mudstone color the deeply eroded fingers of Kutz Canyon, a sight that is most striking at dusk when the setting sun brings out hues of red, purple, and blue.

The exposed canyon walls reveal a story that is millions of years old. Where there is now only rock and dirt, there were once rushing rivers, grasslands, marshes, lakes, and thick forests. Fossil records indicate that turtles and crocodiles, as well as fish, lizards, and mammals, once thrived here.

As the landscape suggests, Angel Peak and the surrounding area is prone to extreme weather. Snow in the winter, searing heat in the summer, and strong canyon winds in almost any season can be expected here. Steep drop-offs, loose rocks along

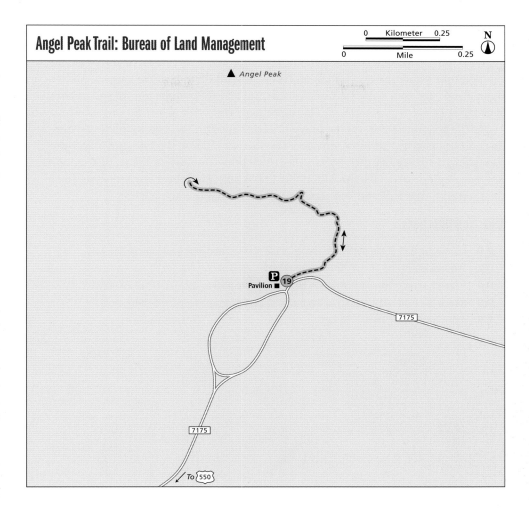

0   Kilometer   0.25

N

0   Mile   0.25

▲ *Angel Peak*

P

19

Pavilion ■

7175

7175

To 550

the rim, and rattlesnakes are other potential hazards. Pay attention to where you step and you'll be fine! Additionally, as in much of New Mexico's public land, there are several operating pumpjacks and other oil field machinery here. Stay well away from this machinery.

There is a (free) campground here, along with sheltered picnic facilities, grills, and vault toilets. No water is available.

While there are lots of opportunities for off-trail or dispersed hiking here, there are basically two trails. A short nature trail connects two picnic areas. The trail described here is more of a worn path that follows the canyon rim and then traverses

◀   *Narrow ridgeline along the trail to Angel Peak*

an exposed ridge into the canyon. It is scenic and dramatic and well worth the trip to this somewhat remote location.

From the picnic pavilion located at the northeastern part of the scenic area and campground, locate the trail leading northeast toward the rim of the canyon. Almost immediately the trail crosses a cattle guard/gate and follows the rim of the canyon east.

At 0.2 mile the trail leaves the canyon rim and turns to the west to follow a ridge-line partway into the canyon. Come to a very narrow ridge at 0.4 mile and follow the path along the ridge between two smaller monoliths. Circumvent the second mono-lith and continue on to the third monolith at 0.8 mile. From here enjoy the view, and then return to the trailhead and parking area via the same route.

Miles and Directions

0.0 Locate the trail at the northeast corner of the pavilion and hike east through the gate.

0.2 The trail leaves the canyon rim and turns west.

0.4 Reach a very narrow ridge between two of the three peaks.

0.8 Reach the third peak. Return to the trailhead and parking area via the same route.

1.6 Arrive back at the start.

20 Farmington River Trails

The residents of the city consider the 2.2-mile trail system along the Animas River in downtown Farmington a treasure. The trails make their way along either side of the river, offer great views of towering cottonwoods, go past the whitewater park, offer access to the downtown area, and even go to a fun little nature center that is nestled quietly in the woods just off the river.

Start: Trailhead and parking area at Berg Park
Distance: 2.2-mile lollipop
Hiking time: 1 to 2 hours
Difficulty: Easy
Trail surface: Forested trail, dirt path, and paved trail
Best season: Best in spring from Mar through May for the wildflower displays and fall from Sept to Nov for the fall foliage

Other trail users: Bikers
Canine compatibility: Leashed dogs permitted
Fees and permits: No fees or permits required
Schedule: Open year-round
Maps: USGS: Farmington South, NM
Trail contact: City of Farmington Parks, Recreation and Cultural Affairs, 901 Fairgrounds Rd., Farmington, NM 87401; (505) 599-1407; www.fmtn.org/index.aspx?nid=198

Finding the trailhead: From downtown Farmington, New Mexico, drive east on San Juan Boulevard for 0.8 mile to the parking area for Berg Park on the right (south). GPS: N36 43.947' / W108 11.219'

The Hike

The network of trails along the Animas River in Animas Park and Berg Park in Farmington is a designated National Recreation Trail. The trails here offer visitors to and residents of the Four Corners region a great opportunity to enjoy the natural beauty of the area in a more urban environment. Walkers, joggers, and bird-watchers will have plenty of opportunities to view wildlife—deer, waterfowl, and fox are often spotted near the trails. The trail leads to several bridge crossings, a whitewater play park for kayakers, and the Riverside Nature Center. Groves of native cottonwood trees, a wetland area, and the Xeriscape Demonstration Garden round out some of the sights you can expect to see along the trail.

Several interesting festivals and events are held in these parks each year, including Riverfest, the Four Corners Storytelling Festival, and Winterglow. There are currently just over 5 miles of constructed trails along the river, but future plans include extending the trails upstream to the community of Aztec and downstream to the town of Kirtland, which could potentially increase the trail system by over 30 miles!

From the Berg Park parking area, begin walking east on the Riverside Trail. At 0.1 mile come to the Riverbend Overlook. The trail forks here. The trail to the left (northeast) is a nature trail. Stay right (east) to continue on to the Archway

Court at 0.2 mile. At 0.3 mile come to a bridge that crosses the Animas River. Stay left (northeast) and do not cross the river (you will cross this bridge on the way back to the parking area).

At 0.6 mile you will come to the All Veterans Memorial. The memorial features a giant, spinning globe sculpture that is suspended in water and details every location where the United States has been involved in a conflict. There is also interpretive information on every major war or conflict involving the United States beginning with the Revolutionary War. Even those with very little interest in U.S. history and the military will find the memorial interesting.

Come to another bridge at 0.9 mile and turn right (south) to cross over the Animas River. Once across the bridge, turn left (east) toward Bird Hollow. Come to Bird Hollow, a great place near a

Animas River

small pond that is ideal for bird-watching, at 1.1 miles and turn right (south) toward the Riverside Nature Center, which you will reach at 1.2 miles. A short trail leading to the nature center breaks off to the left (east). Continue to the right (south) past the Garden View, which highlights a type of water-conscious gardening/landscaping known as xeriscape.

At 1.4 miles you'll reach the whitewater park and cross a small bridge over Willett Ditch to Rocky Reach Landing, and then continue hiking west. Come to a fork in the trail at 1.8 miles. Stay right (north) to return to Berg Park. When you come to a bridge across the Animas River at 1.9 miles, cross it and turn right (west) to return to the trailhead and parking area. Reach the trailhead and parking area at 2.2 miles.

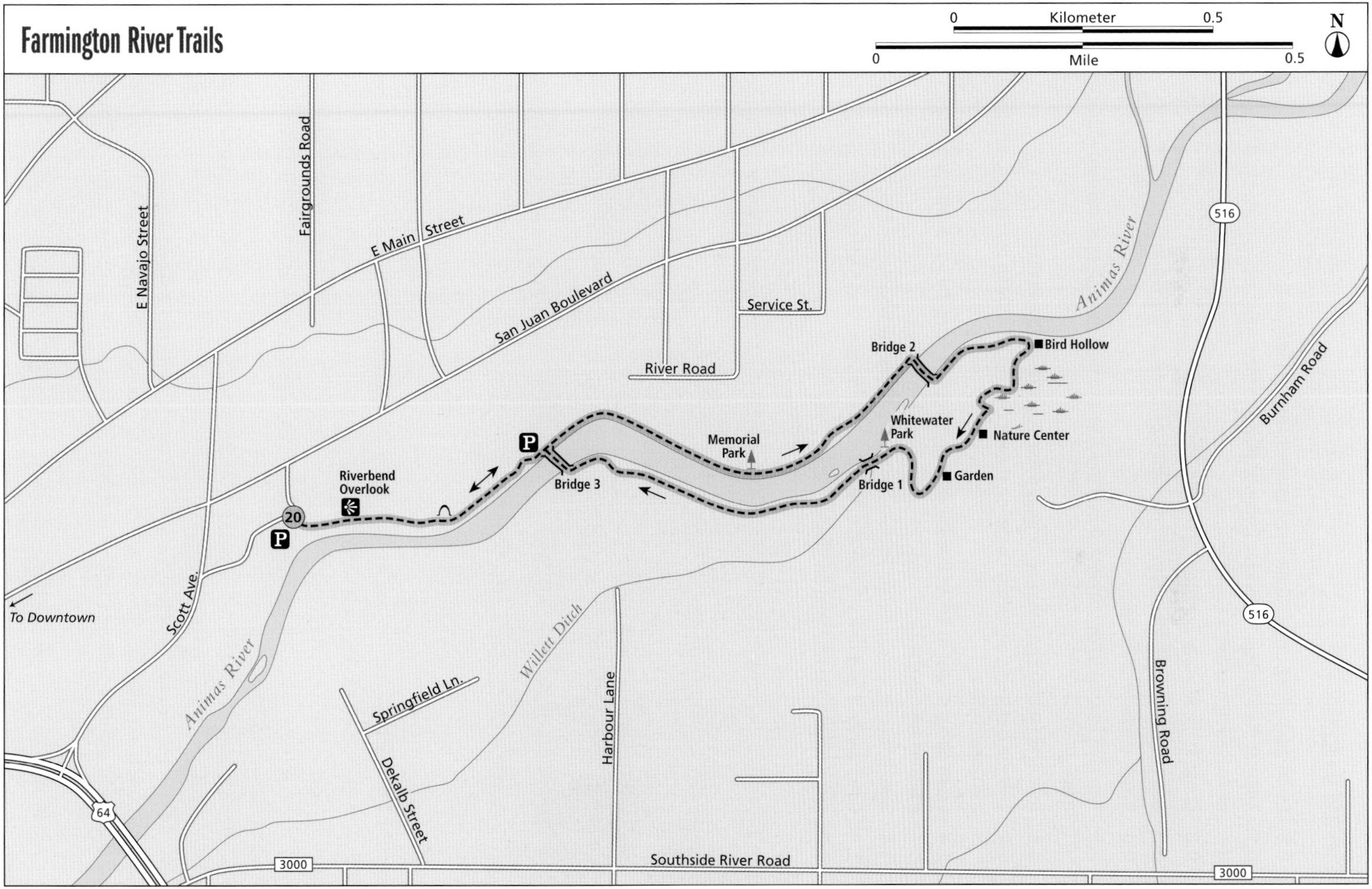

Farmington River Trails

N

0.5 0.5 Kilometer

Mile

Antinas River

516

Burnham Road

516

Browning Road

3000

Bird Hollow

Nature Center

Garden

Bridge 2

Whitewater Park

Bridge 1

Service St.

Memorial Park

River Road

San Juan Boulevard

Bridge 3

Harbour Lane

Willet Ditch

Southside River Road

P

E Main Street

Springfield Ln

Dekalb Street

Fairgrounds Road

Riverbend Overlook

20

P

3000

Scott Ave.

Antinas River

E Navajo Street

64

To Downtown

Miles and Directions

0.0 Leave the parking area and trailhead headed east on the Riverside Trail.

0.1 Arrive at the Riverbend Overlook. Continue hiking to the right (east). A nature trail breaks off to the left (northeast).

0.2 Come to the Archway Court.

0.3 Stay left (northeast). The bridge on the right (south) will be the return trail.

0.6 Reach the All Veterans Memorial.

0.9 Turn right (south) to cross bridge 2 over the river and then turn left (east) toward Bird Hollow.

1.1 Turn right (south) into Bird Hollow toward the Riverside Nature Center.

1.2 Arrive at the Riverside Nature Center on the left (east). Continue to the right (south) past the Garden View.

1.4 Cross bridge 1 over to Rocky Reach Landing on south side of the whitewater park and continue hiking west.

1.8 Turn right (north) toward Berg Park. To the left (south) is the Woodlands Trail.

1.9 Cross bridge 3 and turn left (west) to return to the trailhead and parking area.

2.2 Arrive back at the trailhead and parking area.

21 Penasco Blanco Trail: Chaco Culture National Historical Park

This day hike through the New Mexico desert is a great little getaway. The 7.6-mile out-and-back hike in Chaco Canyon includes petroglyphs, pictographs, Chacoan ruins, and possibly some elk sightings. An early-morning or late-evening hike would be ideal should you choose to hike it in the summer months as the midday heat can be intense in the desert canyon.

Start: Pueblo del Arroyo parking area and trailhead
Distance: 7.6-mile out-and-back
Hiking time: About 5 hours
Difficulty: Moderate due to length and slight elevation gains
Trail surface: Dirt and sand path
Best season: Early spring and late fall for cooler temperatures and wildflowers
Other trail users: None

Canine compatibility: Leashed dogs permitted
Fees and permits: Park entrance fee required
Schedule: Open year-round; check website for closures
Maps: USGS: Pueblo Bonito, NM; trail map available at the visitor center
Trail contact: Chaco Culture National Historical Park, PO Box 220, Nageezi, NM 87037; (505) 786-7014; www.nps.gov/chcu

Finding the trailhead: From Bloomfield, New Mexico, drive 39 miles south on US 550 to CR 7900. Turn right (south) and drive 5 miles; then turn right (southwest) onto CR 7950. Drive 16 miles on CR 7950 to the park entrance. From the park entrance continue another 6.7 miles on the one-way loop through the park, NM 57, to the Pueblo del Arroyo parking area and trailhead. GPS: N36 3.752'/W107 57.934'

The Hike

Chaco Culture National Historical Park is a US National Park Service historical park that is home to some of the most exceptional pueblos in the Southwest. The park is located in the Four Corners region in northwest New Mexico in a remote canyon. It contains the most sweeping collection of ancient ruins north of Mexico and preserves one of the United States' most important pre-Columbian cultural and historical areas.

Between AD 900 and 1150, it is believed that Chaco Canyon was a major center of culture for the Puebloan people. The Chacoans chiseled and shaped sandstone blocks and hauled wood from great distances in order to build what were at the time the largest buildings in North America. The advanced architectural skills of the people are undeniable, as many of the buildings look to have been aligned to capture the solar and lunar cycles. This type of skill requires years upon years of astronomical observations and centuries of skillfully coordinated construction. More than likely

Hiking into Chaco Wash

it was climate change that caused the Chacoans to eventually abandon the canyon, beginning with a 50-year drought believed to have occurred in the 1100s.

The Chacoan cultural sites are fragile, and park managers fear that erosion caused by tourists could continue to damage what is left of some of the ruins. Because of this, some sites have been permanently closed and others may see seasonal closures. The sites are sacred to the Hopi and Pueblo people; therefore, tribal representatives work closely with the National Park Service to share their knowledge and respect the heritage of the Chacoan culture.

To visit the Penasco Blanco Ruins, begin hiking northwest from the Pueblo del Arroyo parking area on the Penasco Blanco Trail. The first section of this trail allows bike riders as well, so the dirt and sand trail is wide in order to accommodate. At 0.2 mile pass the Kin Klesto Ruins and the right (north) turn to the Pueblo Alto Trail. Continue hiking to the left (northwest) toward the Penasco Blanco Ruins. Follow the trail as it travels along the base of the wash wall and eventually comes to the Casa Chiquita Ruins at 1.0 mile. The bike trail ends at this point as well, and the trail narrows to a small footpath. At 1.5 miles you will arrive at a spur trail option. Turn right (north) onto the Petroglyph Trail and follow it as it parallels the main trail and takes you up to the canyon wall for an up-close look at some of the petroglyphs in the park.

◀ *Penasco Blanco Ruins*

Penasco Blanco Trail: Chaco Culture National Historical Park

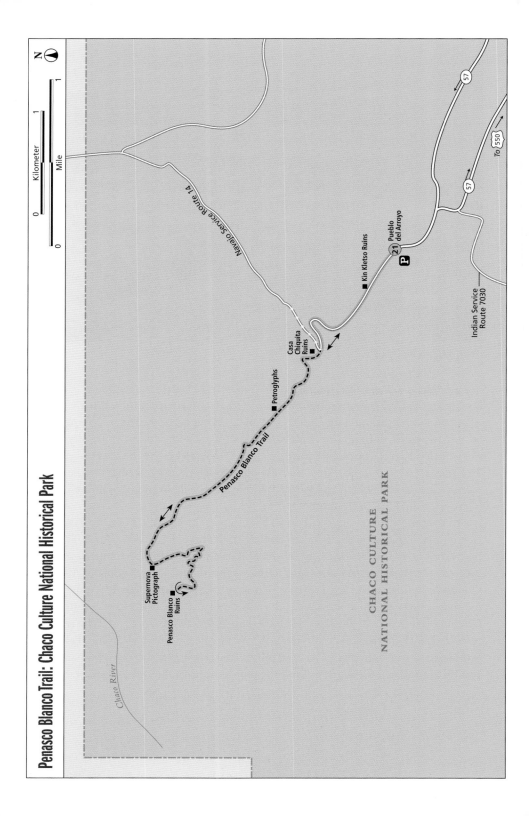

The Petroglyph Trail rejoins the Penasco Blanco Trail at 1.8 miles. Turn right (north-east) back onto the main trail and continue hiking as the trail crosses the canyon.

After crossing from the right side of the canyon over to the left side, you will reach the Chaco Wash. Depending on the season, there may or may not be much water in the wash. Cross the wash at 2.9 miles and then reach the west side of the canyon wall and the Supernova Pictograph at 3.0 miles. The trail turns south and then switchbacks up the canyon wall before turning north again for the final approach to the ruins. Reach the Penasco Blanco Ruins at 3.8 miles. The ruins are large and open for people to walk through. Please respect this sacred area and do not harm any of the ruins. Once you are finished exploring, return to the trailhead and parking area via the same route.

Miles and Directions

0.0 From the Pueblo del Arroyo parking area and trailhead, begin hiking northwest toward the Penasco Blanco Trail.

0.2 Pass the Kin Klesto Ruins on the right (north).

1.0 Come to the Casa Chiquita Ruins on the right (north). The bike trail ends here, and the trail narrows to foot traffic only.

1.5 Turn right (north) onto the Petroglyph Trail to see petroglyphs.

1.8 Turn right (northwest) back onto the Penasco Blanco Trail.

2.9 Come to and cross the Chaco Wash.

3.0 Pass the Supernova Pictograph on the right (west).

3.8 Arrive at the Penasco Blanco Ruins. Turn around and return to the trailhead and parking area via the same route.

7.6 Arrive back at the trailhead and parking area.

22 Pueblo Alto Trail: Chaco Culture National Historical Park

This 5.6-mile lollipop hike is a moderate stroll from the Chaco Canyon floor to the canyon rim. The hike along the Pueblo Alto Trail will take hikers to several scenic overlooks of Chaco Canyon as well as views of a unique set of stairs that have been carved into the canyon wall. Be sure to check the park website for closures that may occur during flash flood seasons.

Start: Pueblo del Arroyo parking area and trailhead
Distance: 5.6-mile lollipop
Hiking time: 3 to 4 hours
Difficulty: Moderate due to length
Trail surface: Dirt, sand, and rock trail
Best season: Early spring and late fall for cooler temperatures
Other trail users: None

Canine compatibility: Leashed dogs permitted
Fees and permits: Park entrance fee required
Schedule: Open year-round; check website for closures
Maps: USGS: Pueblo Bonito, NM; trail map available at the visitor center
Trail contact: Chaco Culture National Historical Park, PO Box 220, Nageezi, NM 87037; (505) 786-7014; www.nps.gov/chcu

Finding the trailhead: From Bloomfield, New Mexico, drive 39 miles south on US 550 to CR 7900. Turn right (south) and drive 5 miles; then turn right (southwest) onto CR 7950. Drive 16 miles on CR 7950 to the park entrance. From the park entrance continue another 6.7 miles on the one-way loop through the park, NM 57, to the Pueblo del Arroyo parking area and trailhead. GPS: N36 3.752'/W107 57.934'

The Hike

Between AD 900 and 1150, it is believed that Chaco Canyon was a major center of culture for the Puebloan people. The Chacoans chiseled and shaped sandstone blocks and hauled wood from great distances in order to build what were at the time the largest buildings in North America. The advanced architectural skills of the people are undeniable, as many of the buildings look to have been aligned to capture the solar and lunar cycles. This type of skill requires years upon years of astronomical observations and centuries of skillfully coordinated construction. More than likely it was climate change that caused the Chacoans to eventually abandon the canyon, beginning with a fifty-year drought believed to have occurred in the 1100s.

Chaco Culture National Historical Park is a US National Park Service historical park that is home to some of the most exceptional pueblos in the Southwest. The

Ruins along the trail

Chaco Canyon

park is located in the Four Corners region in northwest New Mexico in a remote canyon. It contains the most sweeping collection of ancient ruins north of Mexico and preserves one of the United States' most important pre-Columbian cultural and historical areas.

The Chacoan cultural sites are fragile, and park managers fear that erosion caused by tourists could continue to damage what is left of some of the ruins. Because of this, some sites have been permanently closed and others may see seasonal closures. The sites are sacred to the Hopi and Pueblo people; therefore, tribal representatives work closely with the National Park Service to share their knowledge and respect the heritage of the Chacoan culture.

To visit the Pueblo Alto Ruins, begin hiking northwest from the Pueblo del Arroyo parking area on the Pueblo Blanco Trail. The first section of this trail allows bike riders as well, so the dirt and sand trail is wide in order to accommodate. At 0.2 mile come to the Kin Klesto Ruins and the right (north) turn onto the Pueblo Alto Trail. Begin hiking up a rocky section of trail that looks like it will go right up to the canyon wall and end but actually passes through a narrow passageway where a large slab of sandstone has broken away from the main wall. After making your way up through the passage, follow the trail as it travels southeast along the rim of Chaco Canyon. At 1.1 miles you will come to the Pueblo Bonito Overlook and turn left (northeast) onto the Pueblo Alto Trail to begin the loop portion of the hike. The trail continues northeast higher and higher onto the mesa top, climbing over the

Pueblo Alto Trail: Chaco Culture National Historical Park

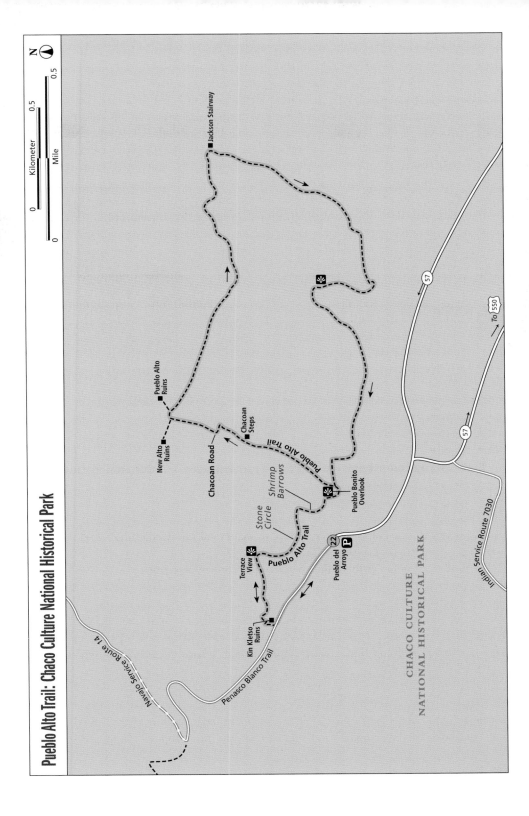

Navajo Service Route 14

Penasco Blanco Trail

Kin Kletso Ruins

Terrace View

Stone Circle

Pueblo Alto Trail

Shrimp Barrows

Pueblo Bonito Overlook

Pueblo del Arroyo

22

Pueblo Alto Ruins

New Alto Ruins

Chacoan Road

Chacoan Steps

Pueblo Alto Trail

Jackson Stairway

57

57

To 550

Indian Service Route 7030

CHACO CULTURE
NATIONAL HISTORICAL PARK

N

Kilometer

0   0.5   0.5

Mile

0   0.5

sandstone benches. At 1.4 miles reach the Chacoan Steps. Archaeologists uncovered these steps back in the 1970s and came to the conclusion that they had simply been carved out by the Chacoans to make travel back and forth easier.

You will arrive at the first set of ruins at 1.7 miles. On the left (west) are the New Alto Ruins, and then at 1.8 miles to the north are the Pueblo Alto Ruins. From the Pueblo Alto Ruins, the trail turns southeast and begins to make its way back to the Chaco Canyon rim, which you will continue to hike along until you reach the Jackson Stairway at 2.7 miles. The stairway was carved into the canyon wall for access from the canyon floor up to the rim. You probably won't be too interested in trying them out when you see them! After the Jackson Stairway the trail turns south and then southwest to drop down onto a lower shelf along the canyon rim before turning northwest and making its way back to the trailhead. On the return you will arrive at a great overlook for Pueblo Bonito on the canyon floor below at 3.7 miles and then reach the end of the loop portion of the hike at 4.5 miles. Stay left (northwest) to return to the trailhead and parking area at 5.6 miles.

Miles and Directions

0.0 From the Pueblo del Arroyo parking area and trailhead, begin hiking northwest on the Pueblo Blanco Trail.

0.2 Turn right (northeast) at the Kin Klesto Ruins and then stay right (northeast) on the Pueblo Alto Trail.

1.1 Come to the Pueblo Bonito Overlook and turn left (northeast) on the Pueblo Alto Trail to begin the loop portion of the hike.

1.4 Reach the Chacoan Steps.

1.7 Reach a spur trail to the left (west) to the New Alto Ruins.

1.8 Reach a spur trail to the left (north) to the Pueblo Alto Ruins.

2.7 Come to the Jackson Stairway.

3.7 Come to an overlook area for Pueblo Bonito.

4.5 The loop portion of the trail ends. Stay left (northwest) to return to the trailhead and parking area.

5.6 Arrive back at the trailhead and parking area.

23 Bisti De-Na-Zin Wilderness: Bureau of Land Management

This 4-mile out-and-back hike in the Bisti De-Na-Zin Wilderness Area will have you wondering, "How did I get here?" The Bisti is full of mystery and wonder and will keep hikers, adventurers, rock hounds, and history buffs busy for hours and even days. The area is a hidden treasure in northwestern New Mexico that locals have been able to keep to themselves for many years. Be sure to take plenty of water for your trip.

Start: Bisti De-Na-Zin Wilderness parking area and trailhead
Distance: 4.0-mile out-and-back
Hiking time: 2 to 3 hours
Difficulty: Easy
Trail surface: Sand and dirt wash
Best season: Spring and fall for cooler temperatures
Other trail users: None
Canine compatibility: Leashed dogs permitted

Fees and permits: No fees or permits required
Schedule: Open year-round
Maps: USGS: Alamo Mesa East, NM
Trail contact: Bureau of Land Management, Farmington Field Office, 6251 College Blvd., Ste. A, Farmington, NM 87402; (505) 564-7600; www.blm.gov/nm/st/en/prog/blm_special_areas/wilderness_and_wsas/wilderness_areas/bisti.html

Finding the trailhead: From Farmington, New Mexico, drive 43.5 miles south on NM 371 to CR 7500. Turn left (east) and drive 13.5 miles to the Bisti De-Na-Zin Wilderness Area parking and trailhead on the left (north). GPS: N36 18.738'/W108 0.168'

The Hike

Get ready for an adventure on this hike! The Bisti De-Na-Zin Wilderness is an other-worldly place located 40 miles south of Farmington. Managed by the Bureau of Land Management, the area consists of 41,170 acres of badlands.

Sandstone, shale, and mudstone, along with coal and silt, make up the majority of the geological features here. The incredible sandstone rock spires, or hoodoos, are the result of weathering and erosion. Rock colors range from maroon to gray to yellow and turn vivid shades of red, purple, and blue at sunset. In addition to the awe-inspiring geology of the area, there is also a rich cultural and paleontological history. Petroglyphs depicting cranes have been found near here, as well as petrified logs and dinosaur fossils. One thing the area does not have is a lot of trails. There are several trailheads, but visitors should be ready to use basic route-finding techniques, along with GPS or map and compass skills.

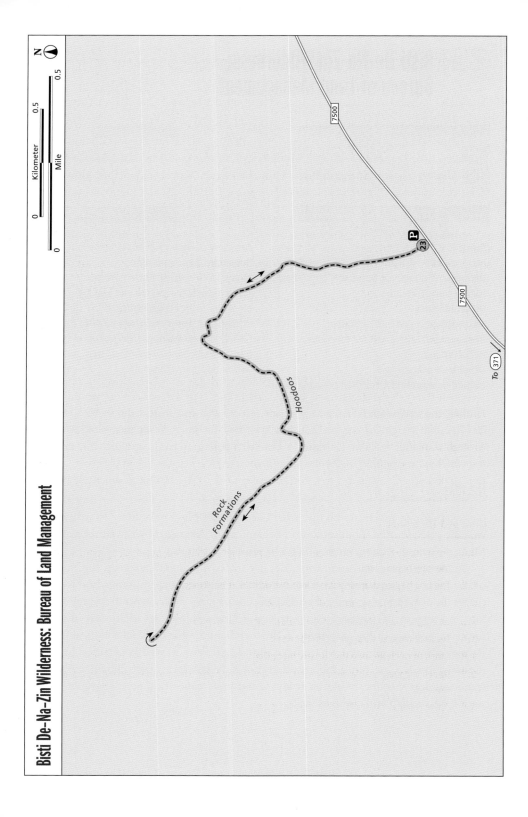

Bisti De–Na–Zin Wilderness: Bureau of Land Management

Rock Formations

Hoodoos

7500

7500

To 371

P

23

Kilometer
0   0.5

Mile
0   0.5

N

Bisti Badlands

From the Bisti De-Na-Zin Wilderness Area parking lot and trailhead, begin hiking north through the sagebrush plain. At 0.2 mile the trail drops down into the wash and enters the badlands. Turn left (southwest) at 0.7 mile and follow the wash. At 1.2 miles turn right (northwest) and follow the trail up and out of the wash. Cross through a smaller wash at 1.4 miles. Come to a pale gray landscape that can only be described as "moonlike" and continue northwest. At 2.0 miles reach a grassland area. This makes a good spot to turn around and return to the trailhead and parking area via the same route.

Miles and Directions

0.0 From the Bisti De-Na-Zin Wilderness Area parking and trailhead, begin hiking north across the sagebrush plain.

0.2 The trail begins dropping down into the wash and badlands.

0.7 Turn left (southwest) and walk in the wash.

1.2 Turn right (northwest) and follow the trail up out of the wash.

1.4 The trail crosses through a smaller wash.

1.8 Cross through an area that is very moonlike.

2.0 Reach a grassy prairie. Turn around here and retrace your steps to the parking area and trailhead.

4.0 Arrive back at the trailhead and parking area.

Storm moving over Bisti De-Na-Zin Wilderness

24 Bisti Badlands: Bureau of Land Management

Follow this out-and-back "trail" through some of the most unique scenery that New Mexico has to offer. The Bisti Badlands do not have designated trails. They are an adventurer's dream! This 6-mile out-and-back hike gives a good sampling of what the area has to offer and should be considered as a starting point to however long you'd like to make your adventure in the area. Don't expect to see too many other hikers.

Start: Bisti Badlands parking access and trailhead
Distance: 6.0-mile out-and-back
Hiking time: 4 hours or more
Difficulty: Easy
Trail surface: Sand and dirt wash
Best season: Spring and fall for cooler temperatures
Other trail users: None
Canine compatibility: Leashed dogs permitted

Fees and permits: No fees or permits required
Schedule: Open year-round
Maps: USGS: Alamo Mesa East, NM
Trail contact: Bureau of Land Management, Farmington Field Office, 6251 College Blvd., Ste. A, Farmington, NM 87402; (505) 564-7600; www.blm.gov/nm/st/en/prog/blm_special_areas/wilderness_and_wsas/wilderness_areas/bisti.html

Finding the trailhead: From Farmington, New Mexico, drive 36.5 miles south on NM 371 to CR 7297. Turn left (east) and drive 1.8 miles to a T-intersection. Turn left (north) at the T and drive another 1.2 miles on CR 7290 to the parking area and trailhead on the right (east). GPS: N36 15.731' / W108 15.170'

The Hike

Be sure to bring plenty of food and water for this hike. If you have an ounce of adventure in your blood, you could spend hours and even days in this area. Dinosaur fossils, petrified trees, and hoodoos are just the beginning of what you'll find in the Bisti Badlands.

From the parking area begin hiking east into the large wash. The wash is at least 100 yards wide, and there is no defined trail through it. As far as that goes, there is not a defined trail for this entire hike. The Bisti Badlands are a completely undeveloped area, and very few actual trails exist since most of the exploring occurs in the washes. If you are familiar with desert hiking at all, then you'll know that when someone talks about a trail in a wash, they actually mean that the wash is the trail. Make sense? At 0.7 mile turn right (south) into the large side wash and begin hiking along the base of the wash wall. There are numerous rock formations, hoodoos, and side canyons to explore here.

As you continue to follow the wash wall, the wash begins to narrow into a slot canyon and eventually dead-ends at 1.4 miles. Turn here and start your return to the

Explore at will in the Bisti Badlands.

main wash by following the east side of the wash wall back out. Turn right (east) at 1.7 miles to quickly explore the opening of this side wash that has several unique hoodoos. Return to the main wash at 2.4 miles and turn right to continue exploring down the large wash. At 3.0 miles you will reach a large open "field" of small hoodoos. The area feels very moonlike. Turn around here and return to the parking area and trailhead via the same route, or feel free to keep exploring. You could literally spend days checking things out here. It's possible to get lost in some of the side washes, but as long as you use the main wash as a handrail and have a decent sense of direction, you should be fine.

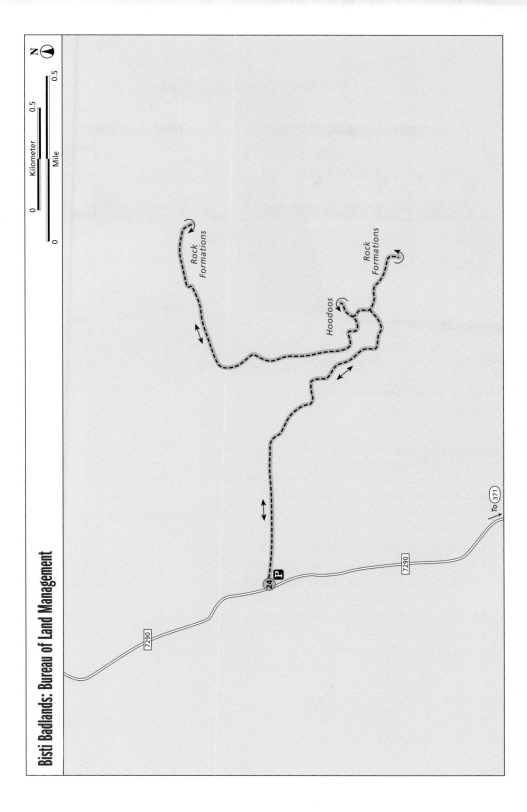

Bisti Badlands: Bureau of Land Management

Small hoodoo

Miles and Directions

0.0 From the parking area begin hiking east into the large wash.

0.7 Turn right (south) into the large side wash.

1.4 The side wash eventually comes to an end. Turn around to follow the other side of the wash back out.

1.7 Another side wash on the right (east) has really cool hoodoos.

2.4 Return to the main wash and turn right to continue exploring.

3.0 Reach a large open "field" of small hoodoos. Turn around and return to the parking area and trailhead via the same route.

6.0 Arrive back at the trailhead and parking area.

Honorable Mentions

L Self-Guided Trail: Aztec Ruins National Monument

Featuring the largest reconstructed great kiva in the United States, Aztec Ruins National Monument is a small treasure in a small southwestern town. The Monument is located within the city limits of Aztec, New Mexico, and offers a short trail through a beautifully preserved set of ancient ruins. The self-guided trail offers a nice overlook area of the ruins and a walk through the ruins and ends with a chance to explore the kiva. In Aztec drive north on Ruins Road for 0.5 mile to the parking area. Locate the trailhead behind the visitor center. For more information contact Aztec Ruins National Monument, 84 CR 2900, Aztec, NM 87410; (505) 334-6174; www.nps.gov/azru/index.htm.

M South Mesa Trail: Chaco Culture National Historical Park

The 3.6-mile South Mesa Trail is located in Chaco Culture National Historical Park and climbs high on the South Mesa. The trail leads to the Tsin Kletzin great house ruins and offers spectacular views of the surrounding desert and canyon. The trail eventually drops down into South Gap before returning to Chaco Canyon and the trailhead and parking area. From Bloomfield, New Mexico, drive 39 miles south on US 550 to CR 7900. Turn right (south) onto CR 7900 and drive 5 miles, and then turn right (southwest) onto CR 7950. Drive 16 miles on CR 7950 to the park entrance. From the park entrance continue another 7 miles to the Casa Rinconada parking area and South Mesa Trail trailhead on the right (south). For more information contact Chaco Culture National Historical Park, PO Box 220, Nageezi, NM 87037; (505) 786-7014; www.nps.gov/chcu.

N Wijiji Trail: Chaco Culture National Historical Park

The 3-mile out-and-back Wijiji Trail is located in Chaco Culture National Historical Park and travels through Chaco Wash at the base of Chacra Mesa. History buffs will enjoy this hike as the trail leads to the Wijiji ruins. These ruins are thought to be a bit different from the rest of the ruins in the park. They are believed to have been built all at one time instead of through several building periods like the other ruins. There are no great kivas or enclosed plazas here. From Bloomfield, New Mexico, drive 39 miles south on US 550 to CR 7900. Turn right (south) onto CR 7900 and drive 5 miles, and then turn right (southwest) onto CR 7950. Drive 16 miles on CR 7950 to the park entrance. From the park entrance continue another 1.5 miles to the Wijiji parking area and trailhead on the left (south). For more information contact Chaco Culture National Historical Park, PO Box 220, Nageezi, NM 87037; (505) 786-7014; www.nps.gov/chcu.

Utah Region

Welcome to adventure! The southeastern Utah portion of the Four Corners region is an area filled with adventures, large natural bridges and arches, deep and narrow canyons, and towering mountain ranges. Part of the land is Navajo reservation, but a majority of the area is public use. Mountain biking, canyoneering, rock climbing, whitewater rafting, kayaking, horseback riding, and of course hiking are all wonderful recreational opportunities in this region. As in northeasten Arizona, stores and restaurants in the small towns scattered throughout the area can be sparse.

Visitors to the area may find themselves driving and/or hiking in a hot desert environment with little to no water in some places. Be prepared by bringing plenty of water and food into this area if you intend to stay outside and away from the few towns.

The highlights of the Utah region include classic beautifully colored rock formations, a dry and arid climate, ancient ruins, and fantastic canyons that have been carved out of this rugged and challenging landscape over many years. Seventeen of the trails in this book are found scattered throughout this mountain and canyon area. When people think of southeastern Utah, Moab is usually a common city name to be mentioned, and for good reason. Moab is a gateway to adventure in Utah, and even though it is pushing the outer limits of the Four Corners region, we had to include hikes around the city in this guide. National parks in the area that are included in this guide are Arches National Park and Natural Bridges National Monument. Other parks nearby include Capital Reef National Park, Bryce Canyon National Park, Canyonlands National Park, and Grand Staircase-Escalante National Monument.

The other trails found in the Utah region are located on Bureau of Land Management land. Hikers choosing hikes from the Utah region of this guide will find themselves hiking in the canyons of southeastern Utah and along rivers that offer world-class rafting and kayaking. They will also make their way to classic destinations like Delicate Arch in Arches National Park and to less-known ruins in remote areas. Dust off your hiking shoes, grab your climbing rope and gear, load up your mountain bike, and grab all your map sets because southeastern Utah can keep adventure seekers busy for a long, long time.

◀ *View from the White Canyon rim (hike 28)*

25 Honaker Trail: Bureau of Land Management

It's not hard to see why the 4.4-mile out-and-back Honaker Trail is one of the coolest hikes in southeastern Utah. Switchbacking down nearly 1,200 vertical feet from the canyon rim to the San Juan River, the trail offers amazing views of the river-carved canyon. From the rim this picturesque location offers gorgeous views of Monument Valley to the south, and it is located not too far from Cedar Mesa and just down the road from Goosenecks State Park.

Start: Large rock cairn located at the rim of the canyon

Distance: 4.4-mile out-and-back

Hiking time: 3 to 4 hours

Difficulty: More challenging due to elevation gain on return hike

Trail surface: Dirt and rock path

Best season: Fall

Other trail users: Horseback riders

Canine compatibility: Leashed dogs permitted

Fees and permits: No fees or permits required

Schedule: Open year-round

Maps: USGS: The Goosenecks, UT; National Geographic Trails Illustrated: #706

Trail contact: Bureau of Land Management, Monticello Field Office, 365 N. Main St., Monticello, UT 84535; (435) 587-1500; www.blm.gov/ut/st/en/prog/more/cultural/archaeology/places_to_visit.html

Finding the trailhead: From Mexican Hat, Utah, drive 3.9 miles north on US 163 to UT 316. Turn left (west) onto UT 316 and drive 0.5 mile to CR 244 / Johns Canyon Road. Turn right (northwest) here and drive 2.5 miles. Turn left (west) onto an unnamed two-wheel-drive road and drive 1.8 miles to an unsigned parking area on the right (west). A large rock cairn can be seen about 100 yards west of the parking area. A high-clearance vehicle can continue from this parking area to the cairn. GPS: N37 11.314' / W109 57.208'

The Hike

The San Juan River could definitely be considered the Four Corners' river as it flows from southwestern Colorado into northwestern New Mexico and then on into southeastern Utah and even hits a part of northeastern Arizona before it empties into the Colorado River. The river is 383 miles long and drains an area of over 24,000 square miles. It's pretty safe to say it is a major tributary running into the Colorado River. The largest tributary of the San Juan River is the Animas River, which receives most of its flow from the San Juan Mountains. The San Juan River does a lot of meandering through horseshoe bends and windings through the four states. One such example is Goosenecks State Park in Utah. The river meanders for 5 miles through a stretch that is only 1 mile long as the crow flies. Needless to say, the San Juan River is an important river in the Four Corners region as it supplies much-needed water to the area and offers numerous recreational opportunities for boating and fishing enthusiasts.

Narrow trail along steep canyon walls

The Honaker Trail in southeastern Utah was built back around 1900 as a supply route for gold prospectors. The trail starts high above the San Juan River and drops nearly 1,200 vertical feet down to the river. Begin hiking on the Honaker Trail from the large rock pile that marks the trailhead. There is no trailhead sign here and no signage to help find the trail. The trail is well-worn and leaves the rock pile headed west down into the canyon. The scenery from the canyon rim is amazing, not only down into the canyon but to the south as well as you can see Monument Valley from the trailhead. The trail switchbacks down the canyon wall at the start and then hits a long stretch at 0.4 mile where it descends steadily to the southwest. At 0.7 mile the switchbacks begin again for a short distance before you arrive at a picturesque rock outcropping at 0.9 mile.

From the rock outcropping locate the trail to the right and continue to descend along the canyon wall as the trail turns to the northeast. After a steady northeasterly

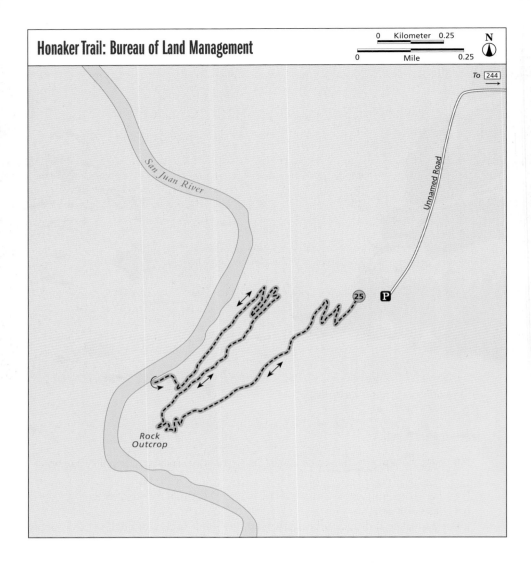

descent, you'll hike down a couple more switchbacks before the final descent to the southwest. Reach the canyon floor and the San Juan River at 2.2 miles. From the bottom the towering canyon walls are mesmerizing and there are a couple of nice sandy areas where hikers can relax, drink, and eat as they prepare for the return hike. Return to the trailhead and parking area via the same route. Be aware that this hike is physically challenging and the temperature in the canyon can be completely different from the weather on the rim. Be prepared.

A large rock pile marking the trailhead

Miles and Directions

0.0 From the large rock cairn on the canyon rim, begin hiking southwest down into the canyon on the obvious trail.

0.4 The switchbacks end for a short distance as the trail traverses the canyon wall.

0.7 The switchbacks begin again.

0.9 Come to a large rock outcropping.

2.2 Arrive at the canyon floor and at the San Juan River. Return to the trailhead and parking area via the same route.

4.4 Arrive back at the trailhead and parking area.

26 House on Fire Ruin Trail: Bureau of Land Management

This pleasant, easy day hike follows the course of upper Mule Canyon, one of the most accessible canyons in the Cedar Mesa region. The 2-mile out-and-back hike travels past great bulging cliffs of Cedar Mesa sandstone that embrace the canyon, which supports an interesting mixture of pinyon–juniper and montane forest environments.

Start: Bridge that crosses Mule Canyon wash
Distance: 2.0-mile out-and-back
Hiking time: About 2 hours
Difficulty: Easy
Trail surface: Dirt, sand, and rocky trail
Best season: Early spring and late fall
Other trail users: Horseback riders
Canine compatibility: Leashed dogs permitted
Fees and permits: Day-use fee and permit required

Schedule: Open year-round
Maps: USGS: Hotel Rock, UT, and South Long Point, UT; National Geographic Trails Illustrated: #706
Trail contact: Bureau of Land Management, Monticello Field Office, 365 N. Main St., Monticello, UT 84535; (435) 587-1500; www.blm.gov/ut/st/en/prog/more/cultural/archaeology/places_to_visit/mule_canyon.html

Finding the trailhead: From Blanding, Utah, follow US 191 south for 3 miles to the junction of US 191 and UT 95. Turn right (west) onto UT 95 and drive 19.3 miles to the signed turnoff for San Juan CR 263 (Arch Canyon). After turning northeast onto San Juan CR 263, pass a parking area and fee station on the right (south) side of the road. Descend a short but rough and rocky downgrade to the bridge spanning Mule Canyon, 0.3 mile from UT 95. A turnout on the right (south) side of CR 263 has room for two to three cars. GPS: N37 32.245' / W109 43.917'

The Hike

The trail in Mule Canyon is sandy but well worn and easy to follow, with few obstacles, making it passable even to novice hikers. You will see several well-preserved Anasazi ruins should you continue to hike farther into the canyon, most of them grain storage structures. The description for this hike leads directly to some of the ruins that are a very popular site for photography—please respect these fragile ancient structures.

From the bridge spanning Mule Canyon wash, follow the obvious trail northwest that descends abruptly to the floor of the shallow canyon. The trail quickly leads to the trailhead register and an informational kiosk. Beyond the register the well-defined trail follows the edge of the Mule Canyon arroyo, soon crossing the usually dry wash to the grassy bench on the opposite side. The canyon is quite shallow at this point, flanked by low walls of Cedar Mesa sandstone. Pinyon and juniper trees cover the north-facing slopes to your left. On south-facing slopes the woodland is open and sparse. After about 0.5 mile, where the wash begins a northwest trend, the canyon

House on Fire Ruin

grows increasingly confined by bulging walls that rise 150 feet to the rims above. Soon, with slickrock underfoot, you begin to follow the floor of the wash. Multiple trails appear frequently in this part of the canyon, but the way is straightforward—you simply follow the wash.

The woodland vegetation in the sheltered confines of the canyon is rich and well developed, more typical of a higher and wetter environment. The northwest trend of the canyon allows considerable shade to be cast by the canyon walls, reducing heat, sunlight, and evaporation. At 1.0 mile you will reach the House on Fire Ruin on the right (north). The ruins are small and sit midway up the canyon wall. House on Fire Ruin earned its name because when photographed at the right time of the day the canyon wall above the ruins looks like flames shooting out of the top of the ruins. During most of the year, if you plan your hike to arrive at the ruins around 10 a.m. and get the right camera setting and camera angle, you can capture the perfect photo. Return to the parking area and trailhead via the same route.

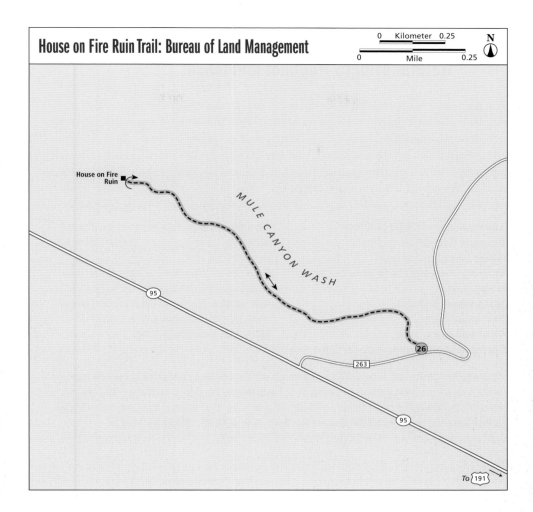

House on Fire Ruin Trail: Bureau of Land Management

0   Kilometer   0.25

0   Mile   0.25

N

House on Fire Ruin

MULE CANYON WASH

95

263

26

95

To 191

Miles and Directions

0.0 From the bridge crossing Mule Canyon wash, begin hiking northwest along the trail.

0.5 The canyon becomes more confined.

1.0 Arrive at House on Fire Ruin. Return to the trailhead and parking area via the same route.

2.0 Arrive back at the parking area and trailhead.

Trail in Mule Canyon

27 Owachomo Natural Bridge Trail: Natural Bridges National Monument

A scenic drive on Bridge View Drive in Natural Bridges National Monument leads past dramatic vista points and several trailheads that access the monument's excellent trail network. Here hikers can follow short, paved paths out to overlooks on the rim, take longer walks into the canyon to visit one of the natural bridges, or utilize the trail network to take loop trips ranging from a half day to all day in length. This 0.6-mile out-and-back hike is an excellent warm-up.

Start: Owachomo Bridge parking area
Distance: 0.6-mile out-and-back
Hiking time: 1 to 2 hours
Difficulty: Moderate due to elevation gain and rocky terrain
Trail surface: Rocky trail
Best season: Any
Other trail users: None
Canine compatibility: No dogs permitted

Fees and permits: Park entrance fee required
Schedule: Open year-round; check website for closure dates
Maps: USGS: Moss Back Butte, UT; trail map available at the visitor center
Trail contact: Natural Bridges National Monument, HC 60, Lake Powell, UT 84533; (435) 692-1234; www.nps.gov/nabr

Finding the trailhead: From Blanding, Utah, drive 3.9 miles south on US 191 and turn right (west) onto UT 95. Drive west on UT 95 for 30.2 miles to UT 275, signed for Natural Bridges National Monument. Turn right (north) onto UT 275 and drive 11.2 miles to the Owachomo Bridge parking area and trailhead via the Bridge View Drive. GPS: N37 35.105' / W110 0.824'

The Hike

Natural Bridges National Monument is a justifiably popular destination, located on the edge of the remote Cedar Mesa in southeastern Utah. The campground in the park makes for an excellent place to spend a few nights and get in some great hiking. It doesn't hurt that Natural Bridges National Monument is considered one of the best places for stargazing due to the lack of ambient light and has even been designated as an International Dark Sky Park.

Locate the trailhead at the northwest corner of the Owachomo Bridge parking area, where you follow the right-hand, unpaved trail, descending slickrock slopes and ledges on a moderately steep grade. The graceful span of Owachomo Bridge soon comes into view in the canyon just below as you reach an overlook at 0.1 mile. The trailside slopes are dominated by Cedar Mesa sandstone and thus host only a scattering of gnarled pinyons and junipers, dark green mounds of littleleaf mountain mahogany, green clumps of Mormon tea, and the spiny foliage of Fremont barberry. Within 5 to 10 minutes most hikers will reach Owachomo Bridge at 0.3 mile. This

Owachomo Natural Bridge

delicate span, with a thickness of only 9 feet, is in the advanced stages of old age. The bridge no longer spans an active watercourse, though a minor draw courses beneath it, just above the drainage of Armstrong Canyon. Surface erosion and weathering slowly enlarge the opening. Many hikers spend time sitting beneath the bridge on the slickrock and just enjoying nature. A few natural stone "benches" can be used for seating. Once you're finished enjoying or exploring the area, return to the trailhead and parking area via the same route.

Option: A 6-mile hike (similar to the Sipapu and Kachina Bridges Loop Trail in Natural Bridges National Monument) combines a trek down Armstrong Canyon, a White Canyon tributary, with a traverse of the mesa-top woodlands and a visit to both the oldest (Owachomo) and the most youthful (Kachina) bridges in the monument. This trip is an excellent alternative to the monument's 8-mile loop for hikers budgeting their time and energy, and it offers a premium return for a minimum investment of time and effort.

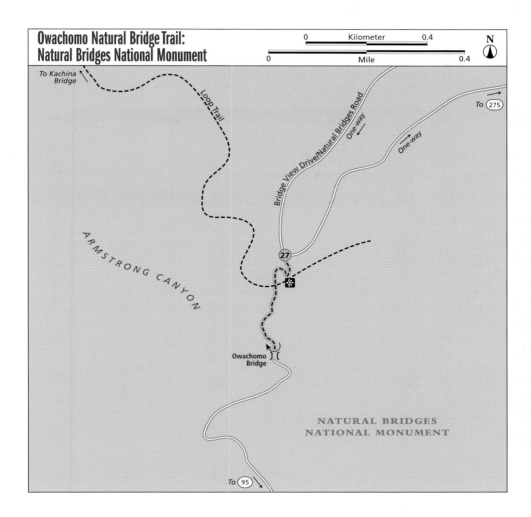

Miles and Directions

0.0   From the Owachomo Bridge overlook parking area, begin hiking south on the trail.

0.1   Come to an overlook area on the left (east).

0.3   Arrive at the Owachomo Natural Bridge. Return to the parking area and trailhead via the same route.

0.6   Arrive back at the start.

◀   *Exploring near Owachomo Bridge*

28 Sipapu and Kachina Bridges Loop Trail: Natural Bridges National Monument

This memorable 5.8-mile half-day loop hike surveys the two largest of the natural bridges in the monument, separated by the dramatic bulging Cedar Mesa sandstone cliffs of White Canyon. The trail passes Horse Collar Ruins, an example of an unusual style of Anasazi architecture, and loops back to the Sipapu Bridge trailhead via the mesa top, giving hikers the entire spectrum of the monument's landscape.

Start: Sipapu Bridge parking area and trailhead
Distance: 5.8-mile loop
Hiking time: 4 to 5 hours
Difficulty: Moderate due to elevation gain and terrain
Trail surface: Rocky, sandy, and dirt trail
Best season: Spring and fall
Other trail users: None

Canine compatibility: No dogs permitted
Fees and permits: Park entrance fee required
Schedule: Open year-round; check website for closure dates
Maps: USGS: Moss Back Butte, UT; trail map available at the visitor center
Trail contact: Natural Bridges National Monument, HC 60, Lake Powell, UT 84533; (435) 692-1234; www.nps.gov/nabr

Finding the trailhead: From Blanding, Utah, drive 3.9 miles south on US 191 and turn right (west) onto UT 95. Drive west on UT 95 for 30.2 miles to UT 275, signed for Natural Bridges National Monument. Turn right (north) onto UT 275 and drive 7.2 miles to the Sipapu Bridge parking area and trailhead. GPS: N37 36.799' / W110 0.554'

The Hike

A visit to Natural Bridges National Monument is a must for anyone traveling on UT 95 across Cedar Mesa. Located near the head of White Canyon, the bridges in the monument are among the largest in the world.

From the Sipapu Bridge trailhead, the trail begins as a slickrock route, descending over the White Canyon rim. The way quickly evolves into a constructed trail, carved into the slickrock, with steps in places that afford better footing. Once below the rim, the trail traverses beneath an overhang to the top of a steel stairway at 0.1 mile that allows passage over an otherwise impassable cliff band. Soon you reach a second stairway that offers an exciting passage over a 20-foot cliff. Just below the stairway you descend a tall, sturdy wooden ladder at 0.2 mile, and then follow the trail as it curves out to a fine viewpoint on a sandstone ledge at 6,000 feet overlooking Sipapu Bridge. The trail then descends steadily.

Descend two short but steep slickrock friction pitches, with the aid of handrails and two short ladders at 0.6 mile, and then reach level ground beneath the bridge in

Trail from Sipapu Bridge to Kachina Bridge

White Canyon wash, about 30 minutes and 0.7 mile from the trailhead. This bridge, the largest in the monument, is no longer being enlarged by stream erosion, since its abutments now rest high above the wash. In its dimensions Sipapu is second only to Rainbow Bridge in Arizona's Glen Canyon National Recreation Area, and thus bears the distinction of being the second-longest natural bridge in the world. To continue, cross the seasonal stream beneath the towering span of Sipapu and follow the well-worn trail southwest, crossing the wash three more times en route to Deer Canyon. The trail ahead is a delightful walk through spectacular White Canyon. Deer Canyon opens up on the right (north) 1.3 miles from the trailhead. Don't miss the short side trip to Horse Collar Ruins at 1.5 miles, just below the mouth of Deer Canyon. A steep, slick rock scramble is necessary to reach the deep alcove that houses an unusual collection of small Anasazi dwellings and granaries.

Resuming your trek down-canyon on the well-defined trail, you will cross the wash five more times en route to Kachina Bridge. Hike under Kachina Bridge at 3.1 miles. The trail continues southbound, now ascending the White Canyon tributary of Armstrong Canyon. At 3.3 miles and just beyond Kachina Bridge is the trail to the canyon rim and the Kachina Bridge parking area. Turn left (east) to begin hiking up the east side of the canyon wall. After a brief slickrock ascent ends, you traverse

Kachina Bridge

a short distance to a signed junction at 3.4 miles. The trail to the right (south) continues ascending Armstrong Canyon, eventually leading to Owachomo Bridge. Bear left (southeast) toward the Kachina Bridge parking area. This trail ascends, steeply at times, via rock steps and a series of short, tight switchbacks. Reach the parking area and road at 3.9 miles. The trail resumes on the opposite (east) side of the road, winding over the mesa top on a gradual uphill. At 4.8 miles turn left (north) at the signed junction, heading toward the Sipapu Bridge trailhead. Turning right (south) will take you to the Owachomo Bridge parking area and trailhead. The trail descends 120 feet into a prominent draw carved into the mesa and then steadily ascends the cairned route across the slickrock. Once to the top of the climb, it is just a short distance to the Sipapu Bridge trailhead at 5.8 miles.

Miles and Directions

0.0 Begin hiking north from the Sipapu Bridge parking area and trailhead as the trail drops down into the canyon.

0.1 Come to a set of man-made stairs to assist with the descent.

0.2 Climb down a set of ladders.

0.6 Climb down a set of ladders.

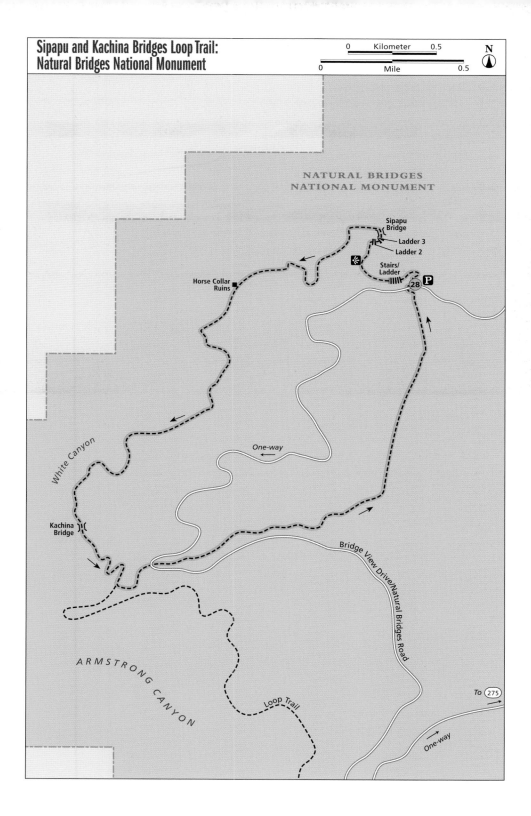

Sipapu and Kachina Bridges Loop Trail: Natural Bridges National Monument

0   Kilometer   0.5

0   Mile   0.5

N

NATURAL BRIDGES
NATIONAL MONUMENT

Sipapu
Bridge

Ladder 3

Ladder 2

Stairs/
Ladder

Horse Collar
Ruins

P

28

White Canyon

One-way

Kachina
Bridge

Bridge View Drive/Natural Bridges Road

To 275

ARMSTRONG CANYON

Loop Trail

One-way

0.7 Reach the canyon floor directly under Sipapu Bridge. Turn left (southwest) to hike through the canyon toward Kachina Bridge.

1.5 Reach the Horse Collar Ruins.

3.1 Continue hiking under Kachina Bridge.

3.3 Turn left (east) to hike up out of the canyon toward the Kachina Bridge parking area and overlook.

3.4 Stay left (east) toward Kachina Bridge overlook. The trail to the right (west) leads to Owachomo Bridge.

3.9 Reach the Kachina Bridge parking area and continue east across Bridge View Drive onto the mesa trail.

4.8 Turn left (north) to return to the Sipapu Bridge parking area and trailhead. The trail to the right (south) leads to the Owachomo Bridge parking area and trailhead.

5.8 Return to the Sipapu Bridge parking area and trailhead.

29 Hidden Valley Trail: Bureau of Land Management

This 4-mile out-and-back trail is located just south of Moab, Utah, and truly lives up to the name "Hidden Valley Trail." After a steep hike up the canyon wall, hikers will find themselves high above the city of Moab just before entering into a hidden valley. The beautiful valley offers access to a network of trails to the south and west of Moab and provides beautiful views of the nearby mountain ranges.

Start: Hidden Valley Trailhead and parking area
Distance: 4.0-mile out-and-back
Hiking time: 2 to 3 hours
Difficulty: More challenging due to steep climb
Trail surface: Rocky and packed-dirt trail
Best season: Spring and fall
Other trail users: Horseback riders
Canine compatibility: Leashed dogs permitted

Fees and permits: No fees or permits required
Schedule: Open year-round
Maps: USGS: Moab, UT; National Geographic Trails Illustrated: #501
Trail contact: Moab Field Office, 82 E. Dogwood, Moab, UT 84532; (435) 259-2100; www.blm.gov/ut/st/en/fo/moab/recreation/hiking_trails/hidden_valley_trail.html

Finding the trailhead: From Moab, Utah, drive 3 miles south on US 191 to Angel Rock Road. Turn right (west) onto Angel Rock Road and drive 0.3 mile to the T-intersection. Turn right (north) onto Rimrock Lane and drive 0.3 mile to the Hidden Valley Trail parking area and trailhead. GPS: N38 31.897' / W109 31.035'

The Hike

Moab, Utah, is considered by many people to be the home of adventure. Adventure is literally within minutes of town, where you will find yourself surrounded by the red rock landscape that Moab is known for as well as national parks like Arches and Canyonlands. Dead Horse Point State Park is just a short drive from Moab and offers amazing views of the Colorado River as it meanders through the river corridors 2,000 feet below. As if that weren't enough, just 20 miles south of Moab are the La Sal Mountains. These alpine mountains are the second-highest mountain range in Utah and top out at over 12,000 feet. All of this amazing scenery and more is what makes Moab such a huge adventure destination.

Downtown Moab has done its part to develop into a place where people can come together in the evening and share their adventure stories from the day or just hang out and shop in outdoor stores and art galleries. The weather in Moab is another influencer, as the winters tend to be mild and the summers are hot but dry, making Moab a year-round destination for people looking to get away. The Hidden Valley Trail is the perfect example of what Moab has to offer. A quick drive south from the

View of the La Sal Mountains from the Hidden Valley Trail

downtown and you are at the trailhead, and a short hike up the side of a canyon wall and you are completely removed from everything.

Begin hiking south from the Hidden Valley Trailhead and parking area on the packed-dirt trail and gradually hike uphill to the trail register at 0.2 mile. Continue hiking west as the trail becomes rocky and starts switchbacking steeply up the side of the canyon wall. The trail climbs high above the Spanish Valley below and quickly begins offering great views of the La Sal Mountains. At 0.5 mile the switchbacks end and the trail starts to level out as it turns to the northwest and enters the Hidden Valley at 0.7 mile. The valley truly is hidden. The city of Moab disappears, and so does all the noise you'd expect to hear so close to the city. Continue traveling northwest through the first part of the valley and hike up the low rise that separates the two halves of the valley at 1.4 miles. At the top of this low rise, you'll drop back down into the second half of the valley and continue to the end, where you'll climb up to a pass at 2.0 miles. Hikers looking to extend their trip can continue west to the Moab Rim Trail. For the current hike description, turn around here and return to the trailhead and parking area via the same route.

Hidden Valley Trail: Bureau of Land Management

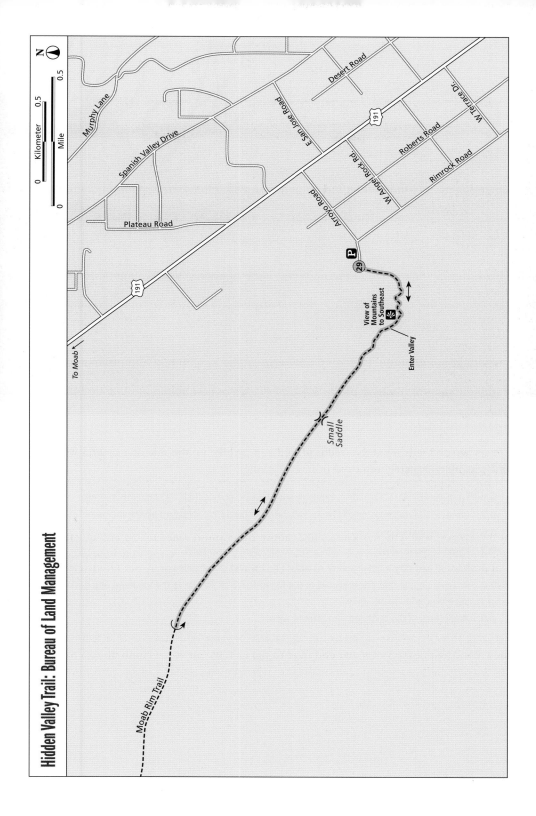

Hidden Valley Trail

Miles and Directions

0.0 From the Hidden Valley Trail parking area and trailhead, begin hiking south on the trail.

0.2 Come to the trail register and begin switchbacks toward the west and up the rock wall.

0.5 The switchbacks end.

0.7 Views of Moab disappear as the entrance into the valley begins.

1.4 Hike up and over a small saddle to enter into the rest of the valley.

2.0 Reach a saddle that offers access to the Moab Rim Trail. Return to the trailhead and parking area via the same route.

4.0 Arrive back at the trailhead and parking area.

Hunters Canyon Trail: Bureau of Land Management

This 4-mile out-and-back hike through a classic Utah canyon offers a great experience for families. The canyon requires no technical skills other than hiking and can be as long or as short a hike as you'd like. The quick access to the trailhead and parking area along with the beautiful scenic drive to get there make this an ideal option for visitors to the area. Watch for mountain bikers, hikers, and runners along the road as they make their way to other trails in the area.

Start: Hunters Canyon Trail parking area and trailhead
Distance: 4.0-mile out-and-back
Hiking time: 2 to 3 hours
Difficulty: Easy
Trail surface: Rock, sand, and dirt trail
Best season: Spring and fall
Other trail users: None
Canine compatibility: Leashed dogs permitted

Fees and permits: No fees or permits required
Schedule: Open year-round
Maps: USGS: Moab, UT; National Geographic Trails Illustrated: #501
Trail contact: Moab Field Office, 82 E. Dogwood, Moab, UT 84532; (435) 259-2100; www.blm.gov/ut/st/en/fo/moab/recreation/hiking_trails/hunters_canyon_trail.html

Finding the trailhead: From Moab, Utah, drive 7.7 miles on Kane Creek Canyon Road to the parking area and trailhead on the left (south). GPS: N38 30.580'/W109 35.801'

The Hike

Hunters Canyon is a great place to get away for the morning or afternoon for a fun family adventure. The trail through the canyon is easy to navigate and very flat. There are campsites at the trailhead and along the first section of the trail, and there is a pit toilet at the trailhead. The drive to the trailhead through Kane Creek Canyon is quite enjoyable as well. Numerous hikers, bikers, and runners make their way out to this area as it is very easily accessed from Moab.

From the trailhead and parking area, begin hiking southeast into the canyon. You'll reach the trail register at 0.3 mile and begin passing the campsites that are dispersed along this first section of the hike. The trail turns south down the canyon right about the time you pass the final campsite. Come to an arch at 0.6 mile that is perched high up on the canyon rim on your right (south). Again, the trail is very easy to navigate through this canyon as the canyon is fairly narrow and there are no side canyons until the trail's end. Pass by two large rock spires on the right (south) at 1.1 miles and then a large alcove about midway up the canyon wall on the left (east) at 1.6 miles.

Trailhead

Just after the alcove you'll reach a large boulder jam at 1.7 miles. Stay left of the jam for the easiest access around it. Some fun rock scrambling is definitely an option here if you are up for an adventure. After the jam the trail and the canyon snake once more left and then right before the trail ends at 2.0 miles. Hunters Canyon runs into three other canyons here. You can see that some people have explored enough in the area to start creating some trails, but for the most part a lot of the trail is undeveloped or overgrown. Turn around here and return to the trailhead and parking lot via the same route.

◀ *Hunters Canyon*

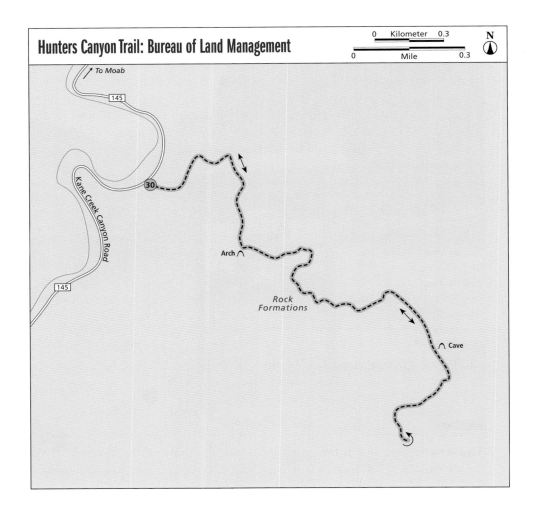

Hunters Canyon Trail: Bureau of Land Management

Miles and Directions

0.0 Begin hiking southeast from the parking area and trailhead.

0.3 Come to the trail register and continue hiking to pass by several campsites.

0.6 Pass an arch on the canyon rim to the right (south).

1.1 Come to two large rock spire formations on the right (south).

1.6 Pass a large alcove opening on the left (east) about midway up the canyon wall.

1.7 Follow the trail to the left (east) of the large boulder jam.

2.0 The trail ends. Return to the trailhead and parking area via the same route.

4.0 Arrive back at the start.

31 Negro Bill Canyon Trail: Bureau of Land Management

The 4.6-mile round-trip Negro Bill Canyon Trail is another gem located very close to downtown Moab. As if the drive to the trail along the Colorado River wasn't enough, the trail takes hikers to the 243-foot-long Morning Glory Natural Bridge. The bridge is the sixth-longest in the United States. During early spring hikers might consider a pair of sandals or water shoes as the trail crosses the year-round stream numerous times along the hike.

Start: Negro Bill Canyon parking area and trailhead
Distance: 4.6-mile out-and-back
Hiking time: 3 to 4 hours
Difficulty: Easy
Trail surface: Rock, sand, and dirt trail
Best season: Spring and fall
Other trail users: None
Canine compatibility: Leashed dogs permitted

Fees and permits: No fees or permits required
Schedule: Open year-round
Maps: USGS: Moab, UT; National Geographic Trails Illustrated: #501
Trail contact: Moab Field Office, 82 E. Dogwood, Moab, UT 84532; (435) 259-2100; www.blm.gov/ut/st/en/fo/moab/recreation/hiking_trails/negro_bill_canyon.html

Finding the trailhead: From Moab, Utah, drive 3.1 miles east on UT 128 to the parking area and trailhead on the right (south). GPS: N38 36.586' / W109 32.014'

The Hike

This 4.6-mile round-trip hike starts just above the banks of the Colorado River east of Moab and travels up scenic Negro Bill Canyon. The hike ends at a stunning 243-foot-long natural bridge, the sixth-largest natural rock span in North America. Remember, the bridge is located in the second side canyon on the right, not in Negro Bill Canyon. One of the best parts about this hike is that the fairly level trail to Morning Glory Bridge ascends just over 200 feet along the way. The singletrack trail begins to the left of a year-round stream that produces plentiful plant life in Negro Bill Canyon, and the steep walls of the canyon provide plenty of shade in the early morning and late afternoon. There is a pit toilet and plenty of parking at the well-maintained parking area.

Begin hiking southeast on the trail through the thick plant life along the creek and reach the trail register at 0.4 mile. In case you are wondering with all this green plant life in the canyon, yes, there is poison ivy in the canyon. Continue along the east bank of the shallow creek. At 1.1 miles you'll come to the first of many creek cross-ings. Not to worry. Unless you're hiking during or right after a lot of rain, the creek crossings are pretty tame. Most of the crossings have well-placed rocks for hopping,

Trail through Negro Bill Canyon

and many hikers will be able to jump over several of the crossings. By the time you cross the creek for the fifth time, you will follow the trail as it turns east at 1.3 miles to stay in Negro Bill Canyon. The canyon to the right (south) is Abyss Canyon. Proceed east in the main canyon as the trail climbs uphill for just a short stretch and then drops back down to the creek to cross a few more times.

At 1.9 miles cross the creek for the ninth time and follow the trail southeast as it leaves Negro Bill Canyon and enters a side canyon. The trail climbs up to a shelf on the left (north) side of the canyon and will continue along this shelf. You'll get your first views of Morning Glory Natural Bridge at 2.1 miles, and after a short distance you will arrive at the bridge at 2.3 miles. The canyon ends here, and the bridge spans across the canyon wall. If you weren't looking for it, you could possibly walk right by it because it blends in with the canyon wall so well. This is a fun place to explore, so take your time and take plenty of photos to try and get the perfect angle of the bridge. Once you are finished, return to the trailhead and parking area via the same route.

◀   *Morning Glory Natural Bridge*

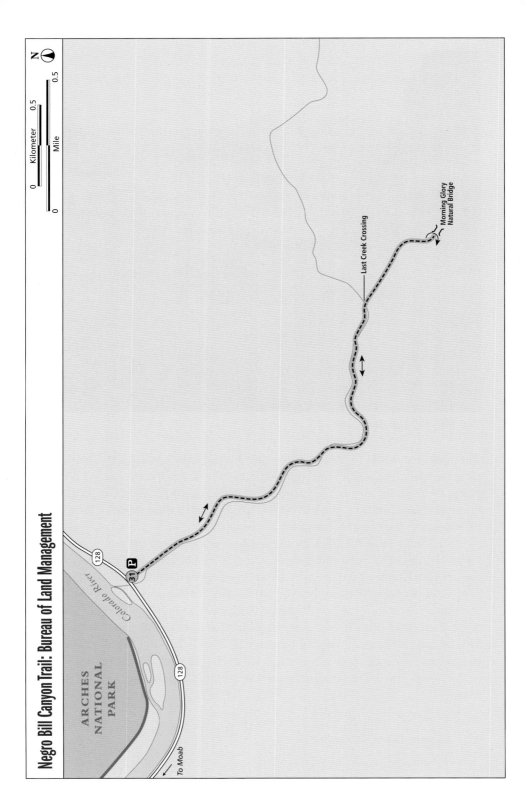

Negro Bill Canyon Trail: Bureau of Land Management

Colorado River

ARCHES NATIONAL PARK

To Moab

128

31 P

128

Last Creek Crossing

Morning Glory Natural Bridge

0   Kilometer   0.5

0   Mile   0.5

N

Miles and Directions

0.0 From the Negro Bill Canyon parking area and trailhead, begin hiking southeast.

0.4 Come to the trail register.

1.1 Come to the first of many stream crossings.

1.3 Cross the stream for the fifth time and then stay left (east) in Negro Bill Canyon. To the right (south) is Abyss Canyon.

1.9 Follow the trail across the stream for the ninth time as it heads southeast into a side canyon and climbs up above the stream to the left.

2.1 See the first views of the natural bridge.

2.3 Arrive at Morning Glory Natural Bridge and the end of the canyon. Return to the trailhead and parking area via the same route.

4.6 Arrive back at the trailhead and parking area.

32 Amphitheater Loop Trail: Bureau of Land Management

This 3.3-mile loop hike strolls out to a beautiful amphitheater-like enclosure. Don't let the start of this hike fool you as you struggle to route-find a bit and walk across a shrubby desert area that seems like nothing will come of it. Once you enter the Amphitheater, the scenery changes completely, rock spires appear, and a large butte rises high from the ground.

Start: Amphitheater Loop Trail trailhead and parking area in the Hittle Bottom Campground
Distance: 3.3-mile loop
Hiking time: 2 to 3 hours
Difficulty: Moderate due to a rock-scrambling section
Trail surface: Rock, sand, and dirt trail
Best season: Spring and fall
Other trail users: None

Canine compatibility: Leashed dogs permitted
Fees and permits: No fees or permits required
Schedule: Open year-round
Maps: USGS: Moab, UT; National Geographic Trails Illustrated: #500
Trail contact: Moab Field Office, 82 E. Dogwood, Moab, UT 84532; (435) 259-2100; www.blm.gov/ut/st/en/fo/moab/recreation/hiking_trails/amphitheatre_loop.html

Finding the trailhead: From Moab, Utah, drive 22 miles east on UT 128 to the parking area and trailhead on the left (north). GPS: N38 45.562'/W109 19.469'

The Hike

The drive alone makes the trip out to the Amphitheater Loop Trail worth the while. UT 128 begins just north of Moab and is known by the locals as "River Road." The highway travels along the southern banks of the Colorado River through a narrow gorge. The towering sandstone walls of the gorge are recognizable from travel guides once you've seen them in person. From Moab to Castle Valley, the Colorado River and UT 128 help to form the southern boundary of Arches National Park. The road has several trailheads and campgrounds scattered along it, and it is not uncommon to come across road bikers out for a ride or mountain bikers riding from one trailhead to the next. Boaters and fishing enthusiasts can be found up and down the road as they access the river from numerous put-in points.

Resorts and lodges can also be located down the road as the canyon opens up several miles to the east. Not surprisingly, many motion pictures and television commercials have been filmed at spots throughout the canyon as well. The Amphitheater Loop Trail is located right next to the Hittle Bottom Campground off UT 128. The campground has tent sites and RV sites and is a regular put-in point for the Colorado River.

Amphitheater Loop Trail

From the Hittle Bottom Campground and the Amphitheater Loop Trailhead and parking area, begin hiking east to cross UT 128 and then turn left (east). At 0.1 mile turn right (southeast) at a rock cairn to begin hiking on a trail that is somewhat difficult to navigate through the shrubland. A lone rock formation sits out in the opening and is the direction to head if you lose track of the trail. You'll reach the rock formation at 0.4 mile and pass it while keeping the rock to your left (north). The trail becomes more obvious at this point, and you are able to see and follow the rock cairns as the trail enters a large wash at 0.7 mile. Continue hiking southeast in the wash as the trail exits and reenters the wash a time or two until you finally enter the Amphitheater at 1.2 miles. It is obvious once you enter, as the towering canyon walls surround you and the large butte that sits in the middle of the Amphitheater.

The trail turns left (east) and begins climbing uphill. At 1.4 miles you will need to rock-scramble a bit up through a tight, narrow passage. The rock-scrambling section ends at 1.6 miles, where you reach the top of the climb and the trail turns sharply to the west and leads out onto a nice overlook area with great views of the Amphitheater as well as the valley to the northwest. The trail eventually turns northwest and begins a slow descent down the ridge. At 1.9 miles you will reach a trail junction.

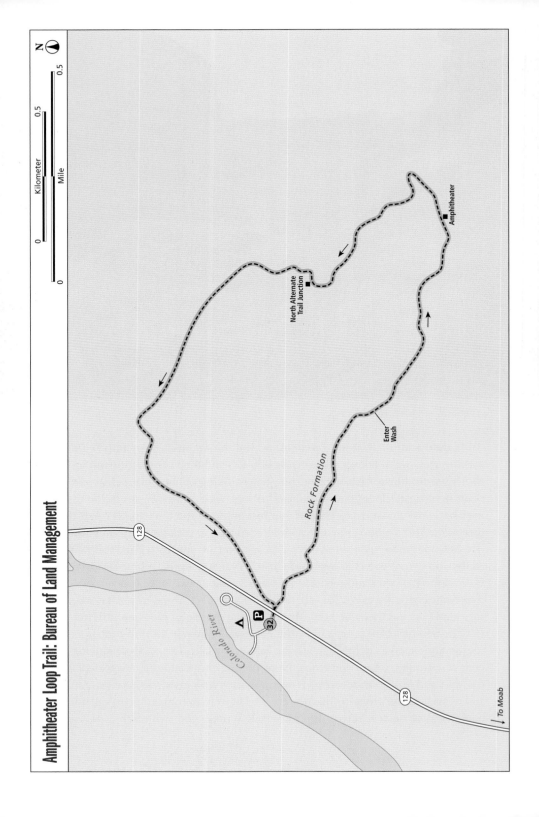

Amphitheater Loop Trail: Bureau of Land Management

View from the trail

Turn right (north) onto the northern section of the loop. Heading left (west) will return you to the trailhead via a shorter hike. From here the trail continues to descend the ridge until you reach the valley floor, and then the trail joins a large wash at 2.3 miles. There are a few cairns along the way and then an arrow at 2.6 miles directing hikers to exit the wash to the left (southwest). Upon leaving the wash, you will find yourself hiking through that shrubby area in which you started the hike except that the trail is marked much better here. Posts with directional arrows keep you headed in the right direction even though you can see the campground and parking area. At 3.2 miles turn right (northwest) to cross UT 128, and then return to the parking area and campground at 3.3 miles.

Miles and Directions

- **0.0** Begin hiking southeast from the parking area and trailhead at the Hittle Bottom Campground and turn left (east) after crossing UT 128.
- **0.1** Turn right (southeast) at the rock cairn to begin hiking southeast on a somewhat tough-to-navigate trail through the shrub brush.
- **0.4** Pass by a rock formation on the left (north).

0.7 The trail enters a large wash and continues in the wash.

1.2 Enter the Amphitheater. The trail turns left (east).

1.4 Begin to rock-scramble up a tight and narrow passage.

1.6 Reach the top of the rock scramble and get great views of the Amphitheater and the valley.

1.9 Turn right (north) onto the northern section of the loop. (*Option:* The left (west) turn returns to the trailhead and parking area.)

2.3 The trail joins a large wash and continues in the wash for a bit.

2.6 The trail exits the wash to the left (southwest). Look for the small arrow sign.

3.2 Turn right (northwest) to cross UT 128 and return to the trailhead and parking area.

3.3 Arrive back at the trailhead and parking area.

33 Corona Arch Trail: Bureau of Land Management

This spectacular hike is a 2.2-mile out-and-back that leads to a very recognizable and well-known arch in the Moab area. The hike requires some rock scrambling in a couple of areas but is still an ideal hike for families. Hikers will also get to see a second arch on this hike, Pinto Arch (Bowtie Arch), that tends to be overshadowed by the size and beauty of Corona Arch (known by some as Rainbow Arch).

Start: Corona Arch parking area and trailhead
Distance: 2.2-mile out-and-back
Hiking time: 1 to 2 hours
Difficulty: Moderate due to a rock-scrambling section
Trail surface: Rock, sand, and dirt trail
Best season: Spring and fall
Other trail users: None
Canine compatibility: Leashed dogs permitted

Fees and permits: No fees or permits required
Schedule: Open year-round
Maps: USGS: Moab, UT; National Geographic Trails Illustrated: #500
Trail contact: Moab Field Office, 82 E. Dogwood, Moab, UT 84532; (435) 259-2100; www.blm.gov/ut/st/en/fo/moab/recreation/hiking_trails/corona_arch_trail.html

Finding the trailhead: From Moab, Utah, turn left (south) onto UT 279 and drive 10 miles to the parking area and trailhead on the right (east). GPS: N38 34.466'/W109 37.940'

The Hike

So many hikes in the Moab area culminate with a big "wow," and the Corona Arch Trail will not let you down if you're expecting that wow factor at the end. However, because of its proximity to Arches National Park, Corona Arch tends to be a little less known. This 2.2-mile trail travels over a slickrock landscape that has been well marked with cairns, making it easy to follow. From the trailhead the trail gains over 400 feet in elevation.

Begin hiking southwest on the Corona Arch Trail from the parking area and trailhead as the trail quickly scrambles up the canyon wall and arrives at the trail register and some train tracks at 0.1 mile. After crossing the railroad tracks north, follow an old eroded roadbed through a gap in the slickrock bench above. Once you reach the top of the canyon wall, follow the trail northeast toward the base of a large sandstone wall. After you reach the wall and follow the base, you'll come to a safety cable at 0.7 mile that protects this slightly exposed section of trail. From this point on, Corona Arch is visible. Follow the rock cairns across the slickrock after the first safety cable until you reach another safety cable and then a ladder at 0.8 mile. This cable and ladder will probably be a little tougher to navigate than the first cable.

Corona Arch Trail: Bureau of Land Management

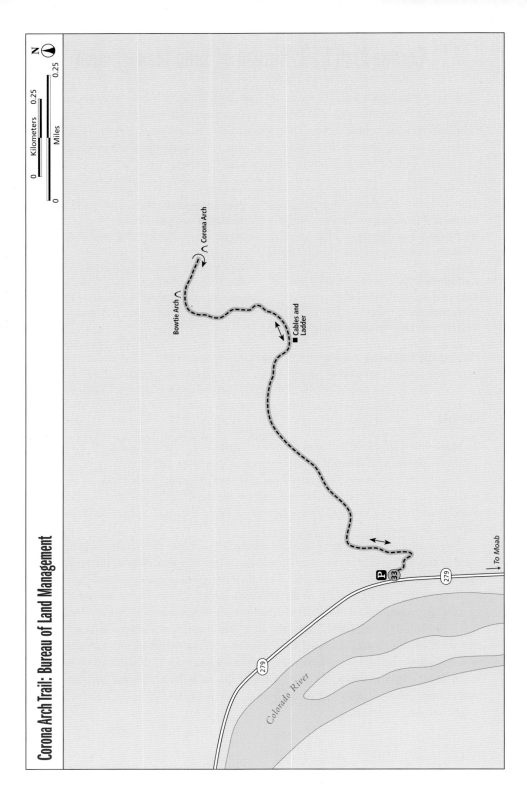

Corona Arch

From the top of the steps that have been carved along the second cable to help hikers, climb the short ladder up over a ledge and follow the cairns up to the top of a large bench. From this point on, the hike is pretty straightforward, with Corona Arch looming in front of you. Before you rush over to Corona Arch, don't forget to stop and check out Bowtie Arch at 1.0 mile on the left (north). Arrive at Corona Arch at 1.1 miles. Once you are finished enjoying the views, return to the trailhead and parking area via the same route.

There is very little to no shade on this hike. Please keep this in mind should you be visiting in the summer. Consider hiking this trail in early morning or early evening. Also, be aware that the cables and ladder will require a certain degree of physical ability.

Miles and Directions

0.0 Begin hiking north from the Corona Arch parking area and trailhead.

0.1 Come to the trail register and cross the train tracks.

0.7 A cable handrail has been placed to assist hikers on the rocky slope.

0.8 Come to a second cable handrail and then a ladder.

1.0 Pass Pinto (Bowtie) Arch on the left (north).

1.1 Arrive at Corona Arch. Return to the trailhead and parking area via the same route.

2.2 Arrive back at the start.

34 Park Avenue Trail: Arches National Park

If you are traveling past Arches National Park and only have time for one quick hike, then this is the one for you. The 2-mile out-and-back hike includes popular rock formations like the Three Gossips, the Courthouse Towers, Queen Nefertiti and Queen Victoria Rocks, the Organ, and the Tower of Babel. All are visible from the road, but there is no comparison to the experience of getting out and hiking through them. All of these natural wonders are famous and oft-photographed.

Start: Park Avenue parking area and trailhead
Distance: 2.0-mile out-and-back
Hiking time: About 2 hours
Difficulty: Easy
Trail surface: Sand, dirt, and rock trail
Best season: Spring and fall
Other trail users: None
Canine compatibility: No dogs permitted
Fees and permits: Park entrance fee required

Schedule: Open year-round; check website for closure dates
Maps: USGS: The Windows Section, UT; National Geographic Trails Illustrated: #211; trail map available at the visitor center
Trail contact: Arches National Park, PO Box 907, Moab, UT 84532; (435) 719-2299; www .nps.gov/arch

Finding the trailhead: From Moab, Utah, drive north on US 191 for 4.6 miles to the park entrance/Arches Scenic Drive. Turn right (north) into the park and drive 3 miles to the Park Avenue parking area and trailhead. GPS: N38 37.465'/W109 35.972'

The Hike

Located just north of Moab, Arches National Park is easily one of the most scenic areas in the world, and people come from all over the world to view this special area—no small task when you consider the park's proximity to a major airport. The park is home to more than 2,000 natural sandstone arches, including Delicate Arch and Skyline Arch.

The Park Avenue Trail follows a dry wash surrounded by giant, red sandstone walls. This short, easy trail can be hiked as an out-and-back hike or can be done as a shuttle hike, since the trail begins at the Park Avenue parking area and viewpoint and ends at the Courthouse Towers parking area and viewpoint. Either way, you will be treated to grand scenery the entire way.

You will probably find that it takes you longer to hike this stunning canyon trail than expected due to all the photo opportunities it provides! This trail does not take you to any of the arches that make this national park so famous, but it will take you

One of the Courthouse Towers

Park Avenue

past several massive and well-known monoliths. This hike provides an interesting vantage for viewing the Courthouse Towers, the Organ, and the Three Gossips, some of the most amazing sandstone features in Utah.

The hike begins at the Park Avenue parking area and trailhead. From the parking area hike north on the obvious dirt path to a viewpoint at 0.1 mile. Here you will have a great view of Park Avenue before you descend the rocky stairs into a dry wash. At 0.3 mile reach the bottom of the stairs and begin following the dry wash down-canyon (north). Come to a slickrock portion of trail at 0.8 mile and watch for rock cairns that guide you along the path. At 0.9 mile the trail exits the wash and continues northeast toward Arches Scenic Drive. At 1.0 mile you will reach the road and the Courthouse Towers parking area and viewpoint. Unless you have set up a shuttle, return to the Park Avenue parking area and trailhead via the same route.

Miles and Directions

0.0 Begin hiking north from the Park Avenue parking area and trailhead.

0.1 Come to stairs that lead down into the canyon.

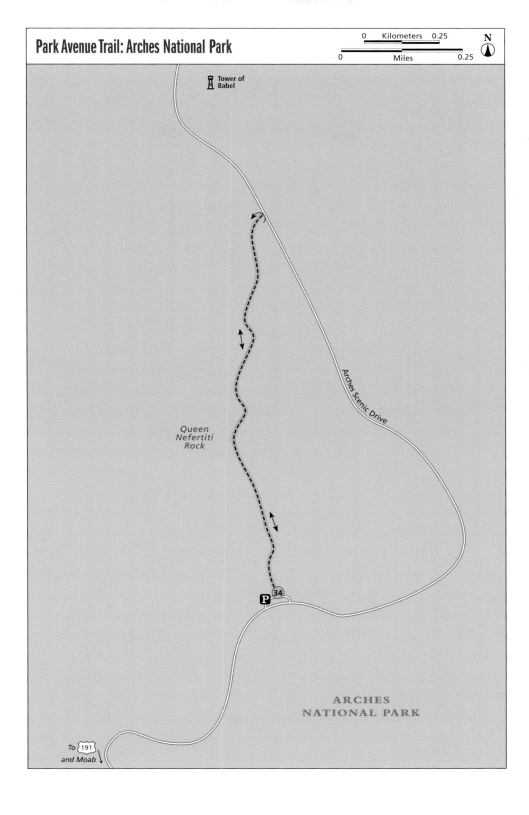

0 Kilometers 0.25

0 Miles 0.25

N

Tower of
Babel

Arches Scenic Drive

Queen
Nefertiti
Rock

P 34

ARCHES
NATIONAL PARK

To 191
and Moab

0.3 Enter a sandy wash.

0.8 Come to a slickrock wash.

0.9 The trail exits the wash toward the road.

1.0 Arrive at the road and the Courthouse Towers parking area. Return to the trailhead and parking area via the same route.

2.0 Arrive back at the Park Avenue parking area and trailhead.

35 Delicate Arch Trail: Arches National Park

This 3.4-mile out-and-back hike in Arches National Park is considered a classic and is probably the most popular hike in the park. Delicate Arch sits 1.7 miles from the trailhead and attracts numerous park-goers because of its sheer beauty and the uniqueness of the arch. The hike includes a long section of slickrock hiking in the middle and at the end, which makes for a fun hike.

Start: Wolfe Ranch parking area and Delicate Arch trailhead
Distance: 3.4-mile out-and-back
Hiking time: 2 to 3 hours
Difficulty: Moderate due to terrain and modest elevation gain
Trail surface: Sand, dirt, and rock trail
Best season: Spring and fall
Other trail users: None
Canine compatibility: No dogs permitted

Fees and permits: Park entrance fee required
Schedule: Open year-round; check website for closure dates
Maps: USGS: The Windows Section, UT; National Geographic Trails Illustrated: #211; trail map available at the visitor center
Trail contact: Arches National Park, PO Box 907, Moab, UT 84532; (435) 719-2299; www .nps.gov/arch

Finding the trailhead: From Moab, Utah, drive north on US 191 for 4.6 miles to the park entrance/Arches Scenic Drive. Turn right (north) into the park and drive 12.3 miles to Delicate Arch Road. Turn right (east) onto Delicate Arch Road and continue 1.3 miles to the Wolfe Ranch parking area and Delicate Arch trailhead on the left (north). GPS: N38 44.138'/W109 31.241'

The Hike

It may not be the largest, widest, or most remote arch in Utah, but Delicate Arch is arguably one of the most beloved and unforgettable arches in the region. Its shape graces the state's license plate, and thousands of people of all ages and nationalities make the 3.4-mile round-trip trek to see this remarkable feature each year. If you're seeking a bit of desert solitude, you might still find it at Delicate Arch—very early in the morning, on a weekday, in the off-season. Otherwise, be prepared to share the trail.

From the Delicate Arch trailhead, begin hiking east toward Wolfe Ranch. Wolfe Ranch is the former homestead of John Wesley Wolfe and his family, who settled in the area in the late 1800s to raise cattle. There is an interpretive trail guide for the 0.25-mile Wolfe Ranch Trail available at the trailhead and visitor center that details life for the Wolfe family as well as the trials of living in the desert. Cross a footbridge over Salt Wash at 0.1 mile and turn left (north) to visit a small cluster of petroglyphs at 0.2 mile. After viewing these interesting petroglyphs—noticing that the art portrays

Delicate Arch

Petroglyphs at Wolfe Ranch

figures on horseback, which gives clues as to when this rock art may have been created—continue southeast to rejoin the trail to Delicate Arch.

The trail gradually begins to climb, coming to a large slickrock slab at 0.9 mile. "Slickrock" is a term that refers to the "petrified" sand dunes that are so common in the Four Corners region. The trail follows a cairn-lined slickrock path until coming to a somewhat narrow ledge. Follow the ledge a short distance before reaching Delicate Arch at 1.7 miles. Take in all the scenic beauty of this special area—where else can you enjoy a 50-foot red sandstone arch and a view of the snow-capped La Sal Mountains at the same time? Return to the trailhead and parking area via the same route.

Delicate Arch Trail: Arches National Park

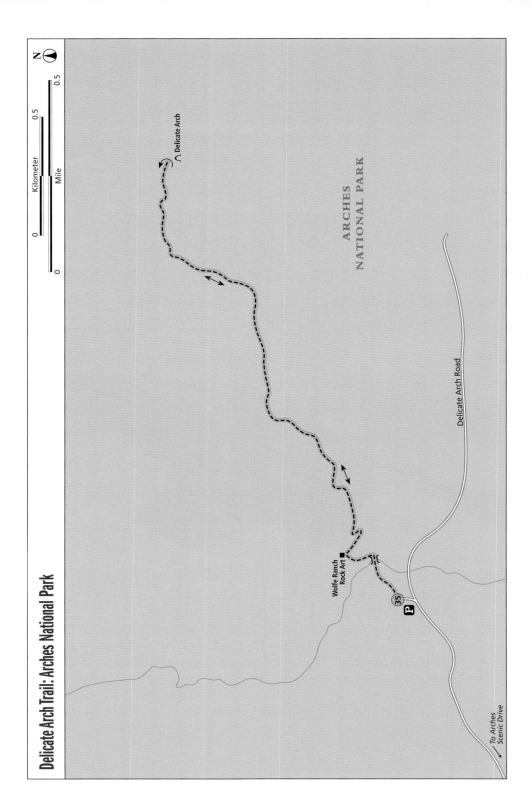

Delicate Arch

Wolfe Ranch
Rock Art

ARCHES
NATIONAL PARK

Delicate Arch Road

35

P

To Arches
Scenic Drive

N

Kilometer

0   0.5

0   0.5
Mile

Miles and Directions

0.0 From the Delicate Arch trailhead, begin hiking east.

0.1 Cross a footbridge and turn left (north) to view petroglyphs.

0.2 Come to the petroglyphs on the left (north).

0.9 The trail approaches and then crosses a large slickrock slab.

1.7 Arrive at Delicate Arch. Return to the trailhead and parking area via the same route.

3.4 Arrive back at the trailhead and parking area.

Honorable Mentions

○ Kane Gulch to Grand Gulch: Bureau of Land Management

Beyond the confines of Utah's national parks, there are hundreds of outstanding canyons that rival those within the parks in their drama and beauty. And among these many canyons, Grand Gulch is one of the finest. Grand Gulch is not only one of the most beautiful canyons in the Glen Canyon region, with its well-developed riparian oases and sculpted sandstone walls, but it also has one of the greatest concentrations of archaeological resources in a single canyon on the Colorado Plateau. This 8-mile round-trip hike from the Kane Gulch Ranger Station to Grand Gulch is a must-do for visitors and locals in the area. From Blanding, Utah, drive 3 miles south on US 191 and turn right (west) onto UT 95. Continue 28.3 miles west on UT 95 to UT 261. Turn left (south) onto UT 261, drive for 3.8 miles, and park at the trailhead next to the Kane Gulch Ranger Station on the east side of UT 261. For more information contact the Bureau of Land Management, Monticello Field Office, 365 N. Main St., Monticello, UT 84535; (435) 587-1500; www.blm.gov/ut/st/en/fo/monticello/recreation/activities/Hiking.html.

⋔ Road Canyon: Bureau of Land Management

Road Canyon is one of a half-dozen major canyons carved into the eastern flanks of Cedar Mesa and draining into Comb Wash. The canyon ranges from 100 to 400 feet deep, embraced by bulging walls of red- and gray-banded Cedar Mesa sandstone that are sculpted into ledges, alcoves, sheer cliffs, and strange hoodoos. A seasonal stream fringed by a ribbon of riparian foliage, inviting benches shaded by a pygmy forest of pinyon and juniper, its sculpted slickrock, and the quiet and solitude provided by its remote, off-the-beaten-track location offer ample incentives for visitors to seek out this canyon. From Blanding, Utah, drive 3 miles south on US 191 and turn right (west) onto UT 95. Continue 28.3 miles west on UT 95 to UT 261 and turn left (south) onto UT 261. Continue for 13.5 miles and turn left (east) onto the road signed for Cigarette Spring. Drive 3.4 miles from the highway and bear left on Cigarette Spring Road; the right fork leads toward Lime Canyon. Continue straight ahead (left) for about 100 yards, and then turn left onto a northbound spur road. Follow the spur 150 yards to the road end and unsigned trailhead, 3.5 miles from UT 261. For more information contact the Bureau of Land Management, Monticello Field Office, 365 N. Main St., Monticello, UT 84535; (435) 587-1500; www.blm.gov/ut/st/en/fo/monticello/recreation/activities/Hiking.html.

Q Government Trail: Bureau of Land Management

Constructed by the Bureau of Land Management in the 1970s, the Government Trail is the second-shortest and easiest access into Grand Gulch. The way follows a long-closed road over the shrub-dotted expanse of Polly's Pasture, near the southwestern edge of the Cedar Mesa/Polly Mesa tableland, and then descends 300 feet via a well-constructed trail into the middle reaches of Grand Gulch. The hike is a rewarding day trip but is most frequently used by backpackers as part of an extended trip in Grand Gulch. Although seasonal water sources are likely to be found in the gulch, day hikers and backpackers alike are advised to pack in an ample water supply. From Blanding, Utah, drive 3 miles south on US 191 and turn right (west) onto UT 95. Continue 28.3 miles west on UT 95 to UT 261 and turn left (south) onto UT 261. Continue for 13.5 miles and turn right (west) onto the road adjacent to the signed road for Cigarette Spring. Continue 2.6 miles to the prominent unsigned junction west of UT 261; then turn right (west). When you reach a signed junction after 3 miles, bear right onto the graded San Juan CR 245. Follow this road for 1.9 miles; then turn right (west) onto a narrow spur road signed for Government Trail. Continue on this road for 1.2 miles to the trailhead next to a willow-fringed stock pond. For more information contact the Bureau of Land Management, Monticello Field Office, 365 N. Main St., Monticello, UT 84535; (435) 587-1500; www.blm.gov/ut/st/en/fo/monticello/recreation/activities/Hiking.html.

R Sundance Trail: Bureau of Land Management

Although the 6.8-mile out-and-back hike on the Sundance Trail into lower Dark Canyon is short, the significant elevation loss and difficult nature of the trail make it one of the most strenuous hikes in this book. It is also one of the most spectacular hikes, affording far-ranging vistas en route to the Grand Canyon–like the gorge of Dark Canyon. A year-round stream flows into lower Dark Canyon from Young's Canyon to Lake Powell. Numerous campsites, most of them shadeless, are between Lean-To and Lost Canyons. The lower elevations of this trip offer access earlier and later in the season than trails in upper Dark Canyon. From Blanding, Utah, drive 3 miles south on US 191 and turn right (west) onto UT 95. Continue 64.7 miles west on UT 95 to the first dirt road after the White Canyon Bridge. After you turn you will see the San Juan CR 2731 signpost. Travel 5 miles on CR 2731 to a Y-intersection with San Juan CR 2081. Turn right onto CR 2081 and drive 3.4 miles from this intersection; there will be a Y-intersection where you do not turn, but the road becomes San Juan CR 256. Stay on CR 256 for about 3.5 miles until you see a wooden Bureau of Land Management sign for the Sundance Trailhead. Continue to the trailhead and parking lot. For more information contact the Bureau of Land Management, Monticello Field Office, 365 N. Main St., Monticello, UT 84535; (435) 587-1500; www.blm.gov/ut/st/en/fo/monticello/recreation/activities/Hiking.html.

S Butler Wash Ruins: Bureau of Land Management

This quick and simple 1-mile round-trip hike is ideal for families. The drive to the trailhead is one of the easier drives in the Utah region, and the hike is relatively easy as well. The result is a rewarding view of some amazing ruins perched high up in the canyon wall of Butler Wash. From Blanding, Utah, drive 3 miles south on US 191 and turn right (west) onto UT 95. Continue 10.5 miles west on UT 95 to the signed parking area for Butler Wash Indian Ruins on the right (north). For more information contact the Bureau of Land Management, Monticello Field Office, 365 N. Main St., Monticello, UT 84535; (435) 587-1500; www.blm.gov/ut/st/en/fo/monticello/recreation/activities/Hiking.html.

T Owl Creek to Nevills Arch: Bureau of Land Management

Nevills Arch is the highlight of this premier 8.6-mile out-and-back day hike. A stream, riparian foliage, deep pools, several pour-offs, and exciting stretches of slickrock walking make this an attractive day hike. Route finding, scrambling, and steep slickrock friction pitches en route down Owl Creek Canyon demand that hikers have previous canyoneering experience. To reach the trailhead from Blanding, Utah, drive 3 miles south on US 191 and turn right (west) onto UT 95. Continue 28.3 miles west on UT 95 to UT 261. Turn left (south) onto UT 261, drive past the Kane Gulch Ranger Station, and continue south for 4.8 miles, turning left (east) onto San Juan CR 253, also signed for Owl Creek-5. The graded eastbound road, which is impassable when wet, is often rocky and rutted in places but should be passable to cars in dry weather, barring flood damage. The road winds over the mesa for 5.3 miles to the large parking area and signed trailhead at the road's end. For more information contact the Bureau of Land Management, Monticello Field Office, 365 N. Main St., Monticello, UT 84535; (435) 587-1500; www.blm.gov/ut/st/en/fo/monticello/recreation/activities/Hiking.html.

The Art of Hiking

When standing nose to nose with a mountain lion, you're probably not too concerned with the issue of ethical behavior in the wild. No doubt you're just terrified. But let's be honest. How often are you nose to nose with a mountain lion? For most of us a hike into the "wild" means loading up the SUV with expensive gear and driving to a toileted trailhead. Sure, you can mourn how civilized we've become—how GPS units have replaced natural instinct and Gore-Tex stands in for true grit—but the silly gadgets of civilization aside, we have plenty of reason to take pride in how we've matured. With survival now on the back burner, we've begun to understand that we have a responsibility to protect, no longer just conquer, our wild places: that they, not we, are at risk. So please, do what you can. The following section will help you understand better what it means to "do what you can" while still making the most of your hiking experience. Anyone can take a hike, but hiking safely and well is an art requiring preparation and proper equipment.

TRAIL ETIQUETTE

Leave No Trace. Always leave an area just like you found it—if not better than you found it. For more information visit www.LNT.org.

Avoid camping in fragile, alpine meadows and along the banks of streams and lakes. Use a camp stove versus building a wood fire. Pack up all of your trash and extra food. Bury human waste at least 100 feet from water sources under 6 to 8 inches of topsoil or 3 to 4 inches in a desert environment. Don't bathe with soap in a lake, stream, or river—use prepackaged moistened towels to wipe sweat and dirt, or bathe in the water without soap.

Stay on the trail. It's true, a path anywhere leads nowhere new, but purists will just have to get over it. Paths serve an important purpose; they limit impact on natural areas. Straying from a designated trail may seem innocent, but it can cause damage to sensitive areas—damage that may take years to recover, if it can recover at all. Even simple shortcuts can be destructive. So, please, stay on the trail.

Leave no weeds. Noxious weeds tend to overtake other plants, which in turn affects animals and birds that depend on them for food. To minimize the spread of noxious weeds, hikers should regularly clean their boots, tents, packs, and hiking poles of mud and seeds. Also brush your dog to remove any weed seeds before heading out into a new area.

Keep your dog under control. You can buy a flexi-lead that allows your dog to go exploring along the trail, while allowing you the ability to reel him in should another hiker approach or should he decide to chase a rabbit. Always obey leash laws and be sure to bury your dog's waste or pack it in resealable plastic bags.

Respect other trail users. Often you're not the only one on the trail. With the rise in popularity of multiuse trails, you'll have to learn a new kind of respect, beyond the

Take extra care to preserve cultural sites.

nod and "hello" approach you may be used to. First, investigate whether you're on a multiuse trail, and assume the appropriate precautions. When you encounter motorized vehicles (ATVs, motorcycles, and 4WDs), be alert. Though they should always yield to the hiker, often they're going too fast or are too lost in the buzz of their engine to react to your presence. If you hear activity ahead, step off the trail just to be safe. Note that you're not likely to hear a mountain biker coming, so be prepared and know ahead of time whether you share the trail with them. Cyclists should always yield to hikers, but that's little comfort to the hiker. Be aware. When you approach horses or pack animals on the trail, always step quietly off the trail, preferably on the downhill side, and let them pass. If you're wearing a large backpack, it's often a good idea to sit down. To some animals, a hiker wearing a large backpack might appear threatening. Many national forests allow domesticated grazing, usually for sheep and cattle. Make sure your dog doesn't harass these animals, and respect ranchers' rights while you're enjoying yours.

GETTING INTO SHAPE

Unless you want to be sore—and possibly have to shorten your trip or vacation—be sure to get in shape before a big hike. If you're terribly out of shape, start a walking program early, preferably 8 weeks in advance. Start with a 15-minute walk during your lunch hour or after work and gradually increase your walking time to an hour. You should also increase your elevation gain. Walking briskly up hills really strengthens your leg muscles and gets your heart rate up. If you work in a storied office building, take the stairs instead of the elevator. If you prefer going to a gym, walk the treadmill or use a stair machine. You can further increase your strength and endurance by walking with a loaded backpack. Stationary exercises you might consider are squats, leg lifts, sit-ups, and push-ups. Other good ways to get in shape include biking, running, aerobics, and, of course, short hikes. Stretching before and after a hike keeps muscles flexible and helps avoid injuries.

PREPAREDNESS

It's been said that failing to plan means planning to fail. So do take the necessary time to plan your trip. Whether going on a short day hike or an extended backpack trip, always prepare for the worst. Simply remembering to pack a copy of the *U.S. Army Survival Manual* is not preparedness. Although it's not a bad idea if you plan on entering truly wild places, it's merely the tourniquet answer to a problem. You need to do your best to prevent the problem from arising in the first place. In order to survive—and to stay reasonably comfortable—you need to concern yourself with the basics: water, food, and shelter. Don't go on a hike without having these bases covered. And don't go on a hike expecting to find these items in the wilderness.

Water. Even in frigid conditions you need at least two quarts of water a day to function efficiently. Add heat and taxing terrain and you can bump that figure up to one gallon. That's simply a base to work from—your metabolism and your level of conditioning can raise or lower that amount. Unless you know your level, assume that you need one gallon of water a day. Now, where do you plan on getting the water? Preferably not from natural water sources. These sources can be loaded with intestinal disturbers, such as bacteria, viruses, and fertilizers. Giardia, the most common of these disturbers, is a protozoan parasite that lives part of its life cycle as a cyst in water sources. The parasite spreads when mammals defecate in water sources. Once ingested, Giardia can induce cramping, diarrhea, vomiting, and fatigue within two days to two weeks after ingestion. Giardiasis is treatable with prescription drugs. If you believe you've contracted giardiasis, see a doctor immediately.

Treating water. The best and easiest solution to avoid polluted water is to carry your water with you. Yet, depending on the nature of your hike and the duration, this may not be an option—one gallon of water weighs eight-and-a-half pounds. In that case you'll need to look into treating water. Regardless of which method you

Ruins along Sand Canyon Trail (hike 4)

choose, you should always carry some water with you in case of an emergency. Save this reserve until you absolutely need it.

There are three methods of treating water: boiling, chemical treatment, and filtering. If you boil water, it's recommended that you do so for 10 to 15 minutes. This is often impractical because you're forced to exhaust a great deal of your fuel supply. You can opt for chemical treatment, which will kill Giardia but will not take care of other chemical pollutants. Another drawback to chemical treatments is the unpleasant taste of the water after it's treated. You can remedy this by adding powdered drink mix to the water. Filters are the preferred method for treating water. Many filters remove Giardia, organic and inorganic contaminants, and don't leave an aftertaste. Water filters are far from perfect as they can easily become clogged or leak if a gasket wears out. It's always a good idea to carry a backup supply of chemical treatment tablets in case your filter decides to quit on you.

Food. If we're talking about survival, you can go days without food, as long as you have water. But we're also talking about comfort. Try to avoid foods that are high in sugar and fat like candy bars and potato chips. These food types are harder to digest and are low in nutritional value. Instead, bring along foods that are easy to pack, nutritious, and high in energy (e.g., bagels, nutrition bars, dehydrated fruit, gorp, and jerky). If you are on an overnight trip, easy-to-fix dinners include rice mixes with dehydrated potatoes, corn, pasta with cheese sauce, and soup mixes.

For a tasty breakfast you can fix hot oatmeal with brown sugar and reconstituted milk powder topped off with banana chips. If you like a hot drink in the morning, bring along herbal tea bags or hot chocolate. If you are a coffee junkie, you can purchase coffee that is packaged like tea bags. You can prepackage all of your meals in heavy-duty resealable plastic bags to keep food from spilling in your pack. These bags can be reused to pack out trash.

Shelter. The type of shelter you choose depends less on the conditions than on your tolerance for discomfort. Shelter comes in many forms—tent, tarp, lean-to, bivy sack, cabin, cave, etc. If you're camping in the desert, a bivy sack may suffice, but if you're above the tree line and a storm is approaching, a better choice is a three- or four-season tent. Tents are the logical and most popular choice for most backpackers as they're lightweight and packable—and you can rest assured that you always have shelter from the elements. Before you leave on your trip, anticipate what the weather and terrain will be like and plan for the type of shelter that will work best for your comfort level (see Equipment later in this section).

Finding a campsite. If there are established campsites, stick to those. If not, start looking for a campsite early—around 3:30 or 4 p.m. Stop at the first decent site you see. Depending on the area, it could be a long time before you find another suitable location. Pitch your camp in an area that's level. Make sure the area is at least 200 feet from

New Alto Ruins (hike 22)

fragile areas like lakeshores, meadows, and stream banks. And try to avoid areas thick in underbrush, as they can harbor insects and provide cover for approaching animals.

If you are camping in stormy, rainy weather, look for a rock outcrop or a shelter in the trees to keep the wind from blowing your tent all night. Be sure that you don't camp under trees with dead limbs that might break off on top of you. Also, try to find an area that has an absorbent surface, such as sandy soil or forest duff. This, in addition to camping on a surface with a slight angle, will provide better drainage. By all means, don't dig trenches to provide drainage around your tent—remember you're practicing zero-impact camping.

If you're in bear country, steer clear of creekbeds or animal paths. If you see any signs of a bear's presence (e.g., scat, footprints), relocate. You'll need to find a campsite near a tall tree where you can hang your food and other items that may attract bears such as deodorant, toothpaste, or soap. Carry a lightweight nylon rope with which to hang your food. As a rule, you should hang your food at least 20 feet from the ground and 5 feet away from the tree trunk. You can put food and other items in a waterproof stuff sack and tie one end of the rope to the stuff sack. To get the other end of the rope over the tree branch, tie a good-size rock to it and gently toss the rock over the tree branch. Pull the stuff sack up to the top of the branch and tie it off. Don't hang food near your tent! Try to hang it at least 100 feet away from your campsite. Alternatives to hanging your food are bear-proof plastic tubes and metal bear boxes.

Lastly, think of comfort. Lie down on the ground where you intend to sleep and see if it's a good fit. For morning warmth (and a nice view to wake up to), have your tent face east.

FIRST AID

If you develop a blister on your hike, you'll wish you had that first-aid kit. Face it, it's just plain good sense. Many companies produce lightweight, compact first-aid kits. Just make sure yours contains at least the following:

- adhesive bandages
- moleskin or duct tape
- various sterile gauze and dressings
- white surgical tape
- an Ace bandage
- an antihistamine
- aspirin
- Betadine solution
- a first-aid book
- antacid tablets

- tweezers
- scissors
- antibacterial wipes
- triple-antibiotic ointment
- plastic gloves
- sterile cotton tip applicators
- syrup of ipecac (to induce vomiting)
- thermometer
- wire splint

Here are a few tips for dealing with and hopefully preventing certain ailments.

Sunburn. Take along sunscreen or sun block, protective clothing, and a wide-brimmed hat. If you do get a sunburn, treat the area with aloe vera gel and protect the area from further sun exposure. At higher elevations the sun's radiation can be particularly damaging to skin. Remember that your eyes are vulnerable to this radiation as well. Sunglasses can be a good way to prevent headaches and permanent eye damage from the sun, especially in places where light-colored rock or patches of snow reflect light up in your face.

Blisters. Be prepared to take care of these hike-spoilers by carrying moleskin (a lightly padded adhesive), gauze and tape, or adhesive bandages. An effective way to apply moleskin is to cut out a circle of moleskin and remove the center—like a doughnut—and place it over the blistered area. Cutting the center out will reduce the pressure applied to the sensitive skin. Other products can help you combat blisters. Some are applied to suspicious hot spots before a blister forms to help decrease friction to that area, while others are applied to the blister after it has popped to help prevent further irritation.

View from the rim of White Canyon (hike 28)

Insect bites and stings. You can treat most insect bites and stings by applying hydro-cortisone 1 percent cream topically and taking a pain medication such as ibuprofen or acetaminophen to reduce swelling. If you forgot to pack these items, a cold compress or a paste of mud and ashes can sometimes assuage the itching and discomfort. Remove any stingers by using tweezers or scraping the area with your fingernail or a knife blade. Don't pinch the area as you'll only spread the venom.

Some hikers are highly sensitive to bites and stings and may have a serious allergic reaction that can be life-threatening. Symptoms of a serious allergic reaction can include wheezing, an asthmatic attack, and shock. The treatment for this severe type of reaction is epinephrine. If you know that you are sensitive to bites and stings, carry a prepackaged kit of epinephrine, which can be obtained only by prescription from your doctor.

Ticks. Ticks can carry diseases such as Rocky Mountain spotted fever and Lyme disease. The best defense is, of course, prevention. If you know you're going to be hiking through an area littered with ticks, wear long pants and a long-sleeved shirt. You can apply a permethrin repellent to your clothing and a Deet repellent to exposed skin. At the end of your hike, do a spot check for ticks (and insects in general). If you do find a tick, grab the head of the tick firmly—with a pair of tweezers if you have them—and gently pull it away from the skin with a twisting motion. Sometimes the mouthparts linger, embedded in your skin. If this happens, try to remove them with a disinfected needle. Clean the affected area with an antibacterial cleanser and then apply triple-antibiotic ointment. Monitor the area for a few days. If irritation persists or a white spot develops, see a doctor for possible infection.

Poison ivy, oak, and sumac. These skin irritants can be found most anywhere in North America and come in the form of a bush or a vine, having leaflets in groups of three, five, seven, or nine. Learn how to spot the plants. The oil they secrete can cause an allergic reaction in the form of blisters, usually about 12 hours after exposure. The itchy rash can last from 10 days to several weeks. The best defense against these irritants is to wear clothing that covers the arms, legs, and torso. For summer zip-off cargo pants come in handy. There are also nonprescription lotions you can apply to exposed skin that guard against the effects of poison ivy/oak/sumac and can be washed off with soap and water. If you think you were in contact with the plants, after hiking (or even on the trail during longer hikes) wash with soap and water. Taking a hot shower with soap after you return home from your hike will also help to remove any lingering oil from your skin. Should you contract a rash from any of these plants, use an antihistamine to reduce the itching. If the rash is localized, create a light bleach/water wash to dry up the area. If the rash has spread, either tough it out or see your doctor about getting a dose of cortisone (available both orally and by injection).

Snakebites. Snakebites are rare in North America. Unless startled or provoked, the majority of snakes will not bite. If you are wise to their habitats and keep a careful eye on the trail, you should be just fine. When stepping over logs, first step on the log, making sure you can see what's on the other side before stepping down. Though your chances of being struck are slim, it's wise to know what to do in the event you are.

If a nonpoisonous snake bites you, allow the wound to bleed a small amount and then cleanse the wounded area with a Betadine solution (10 percent povidone iodine). Rinse the wound with clean water (preferably) or fresh urine (it might sound ugly, but it's sterile). Once the area is clean, cover it with triple-antibiotic ointment and a clean bandage. Remember, most residual damage from snakebites, poisonous or otherwise, comes from infection, not the snake's venom. Keep the area as clean as possible and get medical attention immediately.

If a poisonous snake bites somebody in your party, follow these steps:

- Calm the patient.
- Remove jewelry, watches, and restrictive clothing, and immobilize the affected limb. Do not elevate the injury. Medical opinions vary on whether the area

should be lower or level with the heart, but the consensus is that it should not be above it.

- Make a note of the circumference of the limb at the bite site and at various points above the site as well. This will help you monitor swelling.
- Evacuate your victim. Ideally he should be carried out to minimize movement. If the victim appears to be doing okay, he can walk. Stop and rest frequently, and if the swelling appears to be spreading or the patient's symptoms increase, change your plan and find a way to get your patient transported.
- If you are waiting for rescue, make sure to keep your patient comfortable and hydrated (unless he begins vomiting).

Snakebite treatment is rife with old-fashioned remedies: You used to be told to cut and suck the venom out of the bite site or to use a suction cup extractor for the same purpose; applying an electric shock to the area was even in vogue for a while. Do not do any of these things. Do not apply ice, do not give your patient painkillers, and do not apply a tourniquet. All you really want to do is keep your patient calm and get help. If you're alone and have to hike out, don't run—you'll only increase the flow of blood throughout your system. Instead, walk calmly.

Dehydration. Have you ever hiked in hot weather and had a roaring headache and felt fatigued after only a few miles? More than likely you were dehydrated. Symptoms of dehydration include fatigue, headache, and decreased coordination and judgment. When you are hiking, your body's rate of fluid loss depends on the outside temperature, humidity, altitude, and your activity level. On average, a hiker walking in warm weather will lose four liters of fluid a day. That fluid loss is easily replaced by normal consumption of liquids and food. However, if a hiker is walking briskly in hot, dry weather and hauling a heavy pack, he or she can lose one to three liters of water an hour. It's important to always carry plenty of water and to stop often and drink fluids regularly, even if you aren't thirsty.

Heat exhaustion is the result of a loss of large amounts of electrolytes and often occurs if a hiker is dehydrated and has been under heavy exertion. Common symptoms of heat exhaustion include cramping, exhaustion, fatigue, lightheadedness, and nausea. You can treat heat exhaustion by getting out of the sun and drinking an electrolyte solution made up of one teaspoon of salt and one tablespoon of sugar dissolved in a liter of water. Drink this solution slowly over a period of one hour. Drinking plenty of fluids (preferably an electrolyte solution/sports drink) can prevent heat exhaustion. Avoid hiking during the hottest parts of the day, and wear breathable clothing, a wide-brimmed hat, and sunglasses.

Hypothermia is one of the biggest dangers in the backcountry, especially for day hikers in the summertime. That may sound strange, but imagine starting out on a hike in midsummer when it's sunny and 80°F out. You're clad in nylon shorts and a cotton

Amphitheater Loop Trailhead (hike 32)

T-shirt. About halfway through your hike, the sky begins to cloud up, and in the next hour a light drizzle begins to fall and the wind starts to pick up. Before you know it you are soaking wet and shivering—the perfect recipe for hypothermia. More advanced signs include decreased coordination, slurred speech, and blurred vision. When a victim's temperature falls below 92°F, the blood pressure and pulse plummet, possibly leading to coma and death.

To avoid hypothermia always bring a windproof/rainproof shell; a fleece jacket; long underwear made of a breathable, synthetic fiber; gloves; and hat when you are hiking in the mountains. Learn to adjust your clothing layers based on the temperature. If you are climbing uphill at a moderate pace, you will stay warm, but when you stop for a break, you'll become cold quickly, unless you add more layers of clothing. If a hiker is showing advanced signs of hypothermia, dress him or her in dry clothes and make sure he or she is wearing a hat and gloves. Place the person in a sleeping bag in a tent or shelter that will protect him or her from the wind and other elements. Give the person warm fluids to drink and keep him awake.

Frostbite. When the mercury dips below 32°, your extremities begin to chill. If a persistent chill attacks a localized area, say, your hands or your toes, the circulatory system

San Juan River (hike 15)

reacts by cutting off blood flow to the affected area—the idea being to protect and pre-serve the body's overall temperature. And so it's death by attrition for the affected area. Ice crystals start to form from the water in the cells of the neglected tissue. Deprived of heat, nourishment, and now water, the tissue literally starves. This is frostbite. Prevention is your best defense against this situation. Most prone to frostbite are your face, hands, and feet, so protect these areas well. Wool is the traditional material of choice because it provides ample air space for insulation and draws moisture away from the skin. Syn-thetic fabrics, however, have made great strides in the cold-weather clothing market. Do your research. A pair of light silk liners under your regular gloves is a good trick for keeping warm. They afford some additional warmth, but more importantly they'll allow you to remove your mitts for tedious work without exposing the skin. If your feet or hands start to feel cold or numb due to the elements, warm them as quickly as possible. Place cold hands under your armpits or bury them in your crotch. If your feet are cold, change your socks. If there's plenty of room in your boots, add another pair of socks. Do remember, though, that constricting your feet in tight boots can restrict blood flow and actually make your feet colder more quickly. Your socks need to have breathing room if they're going to be effective. Dead air provides insulation. If your face is cold, place your warm hands over your face, or simply wear a head stocking. Should your skin go numb and start to appear white and waxy, chances are you've got or are developing frostbite.

Don't try to thaw the area unless you can maintain the warmth. In other words don't stop to warm up your frostbitten feet only to head back on the trail. You'll do more damage than good. Tests have shown that hikers who walked on thawed feet did more harm, and endured more pain, than hikers who left the affected areas alone. Do your best to get out of the cold entirely and seek medical attention—which usually consists of performing a rapid rewarming in water for 20 to 30 minutes.

The overall objective in preventing both hypothermia and frostbite is to keep the body's core warm. Protect key areas where heat escapes, like the top of the head, and maintain the proper nutrition level. Foods that are high in calories aid the body in producing heat. Never smoke or drink when you're in situations where the cold is threatening. By affecting blood flow these activities ultimately cool the body's core temperature.

Hantavirus Pulmonary Syndrome (HPS). Deer mice spread the virus that causes HPS, and humans contract it from breathing it in, usually when they've disturbed an area with dust and mice feces from nests or surfaces with mice droppings or urine. Exposure to large numbers of rodents and their feces or urine presents the greatest risk. As hikers, we sometimes enter old buildings, and often deer mice live in these places. We may not be around long enough to be exposed, but do be aware of this disease. About half the people who develop HPS die. Symptoms are flulike and appear about 2 to 3 weeks after exposure. After initial symptoms a dry cough and shortness of breath follow. Breathing is difficult. If you even think you might have HPS, see a doctor immediately!

NATURAL HAZARDS

Besides tripping over a rock or tree root on the trail, there are some real hazards to be aware of while hiking. Even if where you're hiking doesn't have the plethora of poisonous snakes and plants, insects, and grizzly bears found in other parts of the United States, there are a few weather conditions and predators you may need to take into account.

Lightning. Thunderstorms build over the mountains almost every day during the summer. Lightning is generated by thunderheads and can strike without warning, even several miles away from the nearest overhead cloud. The best rule of thumb is to start leaving exposed peaks, ridges, and canyon rims by about noon. This time can vary a little depending on storm buildup. Keep an eye on cloud formation, and don't underestimate how fast a storm can build. The bigger they get, the more likely a thunderstorm will happen. Lightning takes the path of least resistance, so if you're the high point, it might choose you. Ducking under a rock overhang is dangerous as you form the shortest path between the rock and ground. If you dash below tree line, avoid standing under the only or the tallest tree. If you are caught above tree line, stay away from anything metal you might be carrying. Move down off the ridge slightly to a low, treeless point, and squat until the storm passes. If you have an insulating pad, squat on it. Avoid having both your hands and feet touching the ground at once and never lay flat. If you hear a buzzing sound or feel your hair standing on end, move quickly as an electrical charge is building up.

Flash floods. Flash floods pose a threat to those hiking near many of the creeks described in this guide. Keep an eye on the weather and always climb to safety if danger threatens. Flash floods usually subside quickly, so be patient and don't cross a swollen stream.

Bears. Most of the United States (outside of the Pacific Northwest and parts of the Northern Rockies) does not have a grizzly bear population, although some rumors exist about sightings where there should be none. Black bears are plentiful, however. There are black bears in the Four Corners. Here are some tips in case you and a bear scare each other. Most of all, avoid surprising a bear. Talk or sing where visibility or hearing are limited, such as along a rushing creek or in thick brush. While hiking, watch for bear tracks (five toes), droppings (sizable with leaves, partly digested berries, seeds, and/or animal fur), or rocks and roots along the trail that show signs of being dug up (this could be a bear looking for bugs to eat). Keep a clean camp, hang food or use bear-proof storage containers, and don't sleep in the clothes you wore while cooking. Be especially careful to avoid getting between a mother and her cubs. In late summer and fall, bears are busy eating to fatten up for winter, so be extra careful around berry bushes. If you do encounter a bear, move away slowly while facing the bear, talk softly, and avoid direct eye contact. Give the bear room to escape. Since bears are very curious, it might stand upright to get a better whiff of you, and it may even charge you to try to intimidate you. Try to stay calm. If a black bear attacks you, fight back with anything you have handy. Unleashed dogs have been known to come running back to their owners with a bear close behind. Keep your dog on a leash or within view at all times.

Mountain lions. It is extremely unlikely that you will see a mountain lion while hiking. With that being said, mountain lion sightings in the Four Corners do happen. Mountain lions appear to be getting more comfortable around humans as long as deer (their favorite prey) are in an area with adequate cover. Usually elusive and quiet, lions rarely attack people. If you meet a lion, give it a chance to escape. Stay calm and talk firmly to it. Back away slowly while facing the lion. If you run, you'll only encourage the cat to chase you. Make yourself look large by opening a jacket, if you have one, or waving your hiking poles. If the lion behaves aggressively, throw stones, sticks, or whatever you can while remaining tall. If a lion does attack, fight for your life with anything you can grab.

Other considerations. Hunting is a popular sport in the United States, especially during rise season in October and November. Hiking is still enjoyable in those months in many areas, so just take a few precautions. First, learn when the different hunting

Animas River Trailhead (hike 11)

seasons start and end in the area in which you'll be hiking. During this time frame be sure to at least wear a blaze orange hat and possibly put an orange vest over your pack. Don't be surprised to see hunters in camo outfits carrying bows or rifles around during their season. If you would feel more comfortable without hunters around, hike in national parks and monuments or state and local parks where hunting is not allowed.

NAVIGATION

Whether you are going on a short hike in a familiar area or planning a weeklong backpack trip, you should always be equipped with the proper navigational equipment—at the very least a detailed map and a sturdy compass.

Maps. There are many different types of maps available to help you find your way on the trail. Easiest to find are Forest Service maps and BLM (Bureau of Land Management) maps. These maps tend to cover large areas, so be sure they are detailed enough for your particular trip. You can also obtain national park maps as well as high-quality maps from private companies and trail groups. These maps can be obtained either from outdoor stores or ranger stations.

Angel Peak (hike 19)

US Geological Survey topographic maps are particularly popular with hikers—especially serious backcountry hikers. These maps contain the standard map symbols such as roads, lakes, and rivers, as well as contour lines that show the details of the trail terrain like ridges, valleys, passes, and mountain peaks. The 7.5-minute series (1 inch on the map equals approximately ⅔ mile on the ground) provides the closest inspection available. USGS maps are available by mail (U.S. Geological Survey, Map Distribution Branch, PO Box 25286, Denver, CO 80225) or at mapping.usgs.gov/esic/to_order.html.

If you want to check out the high-tech world of maps, you can purchase topographic maps on CD-ROM. These software-mapping programs let you select a route on your computer, print it out, then take it with you on the trail. Some software mapping programs let you insert symbols and labels, download waypoints from a GPS unit, and export the maps to other software programs.

The art of map reading is a skill that you can develop by first practicing in an area you are familiar with. To begin, orient the map so the map is lined up in the correct direction (i.e., north on the map is lined up with true north). Next, familiarize yourself with the map symbols and try and match them up with terrain features around you such as a high ridge, mountain peak, river, or lake. If you are practicing with a USGS map, notice the contour lines. On gentler terrain these contour lines are spaced farther apart, and on steeper terrain they are closer together. Pick a short loop trail, and stop frequently to check your position on the map. As you practice map reading, you'll learn how to anticipate a steep section on the trail, a good place to take a rest break, and so on.

Compasses. First off, the sun is not a substitute for a compass. So, what kind of compass should you have? Here are some characteristics you should look for: a rectangular base with detailed scales, a liquid-filled housing, protective housing, a sighting line on the mirror, luminous alignment and back-bearing arrows, a luminous north-seeking arrow, and a well-defined bezel ring.

You can learn compass basics by reading the detailed instructions included with your compass. If you want to fine-tune your compass skills, sign up for an orienteering class or purchase a book on compass reading. Once you've learned the basic skills of using a compass, remember to practice these skills before you head into the backcountry.

If you are a klutz at using a compass, you may be interested in checking out the technical wizardry of the GPS (Global Positioning System) device. The GPS was developed by the Pentagon and works off twenty-four NAVSTAR satellites, which were designed to guide missiles to their targets. A GPS device is a handheld unit that calculates your latitude and longitude with the easy press of a button. The Department of Defense used to scramble the satellite signals a bit to prevent civilians (and spies!) from getting extremely accurate readings, but that practice was discontinued in May 2000, and GPS units now provide nearly pinpoint accuracy (within 30 to 60 feet).

There are many different types of GPS units available, and they range in price from $100 to $400. In general, all GPS units have a display screen and keypad where you input information. In addition to acting as a compass, the unit allows you to plot your route, easily retrace your path, track your traveling speed, find the mileage between waypoints, and calculate the total mileage of your route. Before you purchase a GPS unit, keep in mind that these devices don't pick up signals indoors, in heavily wooded areas, on mountain peaks, or in deep valleys. Also, batteries can wear out or other technical problems can develop. A GPS unit should be used in conjunction with a map and compass, not in place of those items.

Pedometers. A pedometer is a small, clip-on unit with a digital display that calculates your hiking distance in miles or kilometers based on your walking stride. Some units also calculate the calories you burn and your total hiking time. Pedometers are available at most large outdoor stores and range in price from $20 to $40.

TRIP PLANNING

Planning your hiking adventure begins with letting a friend or relative know your trip itinerary so they can call for help if you don't return at your scheduled time. Your next task is to make sure you are outfitted to experience the risks and rewards of the trail. This section highlights gear and clothing you may want to take with you to get the most out of your hike.

Day Hike

- ❑ camera
- ❑ compass/GPS unit
- ❑ pedometer
- ❑ daypack
- ❑ first-aid kit
- ❑ food
- ❑ guidebook
- ❑ headlamp/flashlight with extra batteries and bulbs
- ❑ hat
- ❑ insect repellent
- ❑ knife/multipurpose tool
- ❑ map
- ❑ matches in waterproof container and fire starter
- ❑ fleece jacket
- ❑ rain gear
- ❑ space blanket
- ❑ sunglasses
- ❑ sunscreen
- ❑ swimsuit and/or fishing gear (if hiking to a lake)
- ❑ watch
- ❑ water
- ❑ water bottles/water hydration system

Overnight Trip

- ❑ backpack and waterproof rain cover
- ❑ backpacker's trowel

- ❑ bandanna
- ❑ biodegradable soap
- ❑ pot scrubber
- ❑ collapsible water container (two- to three-gallon capacity)
- ❑ clothing—extra wool socks, shirts, and shorts
- ❑ cook set/utensils
- ❑ ditty bags to store gear
- ❑ extra plastic resealable bags
- ❑ gaiters
- ❑ garbage bag
- ❑ bear canister or rope to hang food
- ❑ ground cloth
- ❑ journal/pen
- ❑ nylon rope to hang food
- ❑ long underwear
- ❑ permit (if required)
- ❑ rain jacket and pants
- ❑ sandals to wear around camp and to ford streams
- ❑ sleeping bag
- ❑ waterproof stuff sack
- ❑ sleeping pad
- ❑ small bath towel
- ❑ stove and fuel
- ❑ tent
- ❑ toiletry items
- ❑ water filter
- ❑ whistle

EQUIPMENT

With the outdoor market currently flooded with products, many of which are pure gimmickry, it seems impossible to both differentiate and choose. Do I really need a tropical-fish-lined collapsible shower? (No, you don't.) The only defense against the maddening quantity of items thrust in your face is to think practically—and to do so before you go shopping. The worst buys are impulsive buys. Since most name brands will differ only slightly in quality, it's best to know what you're looking for in terms of function. Buy only what you need. You will, don't forget, be carrying what you've bought on your back. Here are some things to keep in mind before you go shopping.

Clothes. Clothing is your armor against Mother Nature's little surprises. Hikers should be prepared for any possibility, especially when hiking in mountainous areas. Adequate rain protection and extra layers of clothing are a good idea. In summer a wide-brimmed hat can help keep the sun at bay. In the winter months the first layer you'll want to wear is a "wicking" layer of long underwear that keeps perspiration away from your skin. Wear long underwear made from synthetic fibers that wick moisture away from the skin and draw it toward the next layer of clothing, where it then evaporates. Avoid wearing long underwear made of cotton as it is slow to dry and keeps moisture next to your skin.

The second layer you'll wear is the "insulating" layer. Aside from keeping you warm, this layer needs to "breathe" so you stay dry while hiking. A fabric that provides insulation and dries quickly is fleece. It's interesting to note that this one-of-a-kind fabric is made out of recycled plastic. Purchasing a zip-up jacket made of this material is highly recommended.

The last line of layering defense is the "shell" layer. You'll need some type of waterproof, windproof, breathable jacket that will fit over all of your other layers. It should have a large hood that fits over a hat. You'll also need a good pair of rain pants made from a similar waterproof, breathable fabric. Some Gore-Tex jackets cost as much as $500, but you should know that there are more affordable fabrics out there that work just as well.

Now that you've learned the basics of layering, you can't forget to protect your hands and face. In cold, windy, or rainy weather, you'll need a hat made of wool or fleece and insulated, waterproof gloves that will keep your hands warm and toasty. As mentioned earlier, buying an additional pair of light silk liners to wear under your regular gloves is a good idea.

Footwear. If you have any extra money to spend on your trip, put that money into boots or trail shoes. Poor shoes will bring a hike to a halt faster than anything else. To avoid this annoyance, buy shoes that provide support and are lightweight and flexible. A lightweight hiking boot is better than a heavy, leather mountaineering boot for most day hikes and backpacking. Trail running shoes provide a little extra cushion that many people wear for hiking.

These running shoes are lighter, more flexible, and more breathable than hiking boots. If you know you'll be hiking in wet weather often, purchase boots or shoes with a Gore-Tex liner, which will help keep your feet dry.

When buying your boots, be sure to wear the same type of socks you'll be wearing on the trail. If the boots you're buying are for cold-weather hiking, try the boots on while wearing two pairs of socks. Speaking of socks, a good cold-weather sock combination is to wear a thinner sock made of wool or polypropylene covered by a heavier outer sock made of wool or a synthetic/wool mix. The inner sock protects the foot from the rubbing effects of the outer sock and prevents blisters. Many outdoor stores have some type of ramp to simulate hiking uphill and downhill. Be sure to take advantage of this test, as toe-jamming boot fronts can be very painful and debilitating on the downhill trek.

Once you've purchased your footwear, be sure to break it in before you hit the trail. New footwear is often stiff and needs to be stretched and molded to your foot.

Trekking poles. Trekking poles help with balance, and more importantly take pressure off your knees. The ones with shock absorbers are easier on your elbows and knees. Some poles even come with a camera attachment to be used as a monopod. And heaven forbid you meet a mountain lion, bear, or unfriendly dog—the poles can make you look a lot bigger.

Backpacks. No matter what type of hiking you do, you'll need a pack of some sort to carry the basic trail essentials. There are a variety of backpacks on the market, but let's first discuss what you intend to use it for. Day hikes or overnight trips?

If you plan on doing a day hike, a daypack should have some of the following characteristics: a padded hip belt that's at least 2 inches in diameter (avoid packs with only a small nylon piece of webbing for a hip belt); a chest strap (the chest strap helps stabilize the pack against your body); external pockets to carry water and other items that you want easy access to; an internal pocket to hold keys, a knife, a wallet, and other miscellaneous items; an external lashing system to hold a jacket; and, if you so desire, a hydration pocket for carrying a hydration system (which consists of a water bladder with an attachable drinking hose).

For short hikes some hikers like to use small, lightweight daypacks to store just a camera, food, a compass, a map, and other trail essentials. Most of these light-weight daypacks have pockets for two water bottles and areas to store cell phones, snacks, and other items you will want to access easily.

If you intend to do an extended overnight trip, there are multiple considerations. First off, you need to decide what kind of framed pack you want. There are two backpack types for backpacking: the internal frame and the external frame. An internal frame pack rests closer to your body, making it more stable and easier to balance when hiking over rough terrain. An external frame pack is just that, an aluminum frame attached to the exterior of the pack. Some hikers consider an external frame

View of Potato Hill (hike 7)

pack to be better for long backpack trips because it distributes the pack weight better and allows you to carry heavier loads. It's often easier to pack, and your gear is more accessible. It also offers better back ventilation in hot weather.

The most critical measurement for fitting a pack is torso length. The pack needs to rest evenly on your hips without sagging. A good pack will come in two or three sizes and have straps and hip belts that are adjustable according to your body size and characteristics.

When you purchase a backpack, go to an outdoor store with salespeople who are knowledgeable in how to properly fit a pack. Once the pack is fitted for you, load the pack with the amount of weight you plan on taking on the trail. The weight of the pack should be distributed evenly, and you should be able to swing your arms and walk briskly without feeling out of balance. Another good technique for evaluating a pack is to walk up and down stairs and make quick turns to the right and to the left to be sure the pack doesn't feel out of balance. Other features that are nice to have on a backpack include a removable day pack or fanny pack, external pockets for extra water, and extra lash points to attach a jacket or other items.

Sleeping bags and pads. Sleeping bags are rated by temperature. You can purchase a bag made with synthetic insulation, or you can buy a goose down bag. Goose down bags are more expensive, but they have a higher insulating capacity by weight and will keep their loft longer. You'll want to purchase a bag with a temperature rating that fits the time of year and conditions you are most likely to camp in.

One caveat: The techno-standard for temperature ratings is far from perfect. Ratings vary from manufacturer to manufacturer, so to protect yourself you should purchase a bag rated 10° to 15° below the temperature you expect to be camping in. Synthetic bags are more resistant to water than down bags, but many down bags are now made with a Gore-Tex shell that helps to repel water. Down bags are also more compressible than synthetic bags and take up less room in your pack, which is an important consideration if you are planning a multiday backpack trip. Features to look for in a sleeping bag include a mummy-style bag, a hood you can cinch down around your head in cold weather, and draft tubes along the zippers that help keep heat in and drafts out.

You'll also want a sleeping pad to provide insulation and padding from the cold ground. There are different types of sleeping pads available, from the more expensive self-inflating air mattresses to the less expensive closed-cell foam pads. Self-inflating air mattresses are usually heavier than closed-cell foam mattresses and are prone to punctures.

Tents. The tent is your home away from home while on the trail. It provides protection from wind, rain, snow, and insects. A three-season tent is a good choice for backpacking and can range in price from $100 to $500 and more. These lightweight and versatile tents provide protection in all types of weather, except heavy snowstorms or high winds, and range in weight from 4 to 8 pounds. Look for a tent that's easy to set up and will easily fit two people with gear. Dome-type tents usually offer more headroom and places to store gear. Other handy tent features include a vestibule where you can store wet boots and backpacks. Some nice-to-have items in a tent include interior pockets to store small items and lashing points to hang a clothesline. Most three-season tents also come with stakes so you can secure the tent in high winds. Before you purchase a tent, set it up and take it down a few times to be sure it is easy to handle. Also, sit inside the tent and make sure it has enough room for you and your gear.

Cell phones. Many hikers are carrying their cell phones into the backcountry these days in case of emergency. That's fine and good, but please know that cell phone coverage is often poor to nonexistent in valleys, canyons, and thick forest. More important, people have started to call for help because they're tired or lost. Let's go back to being prepared. You are responsible for yourself in the backcountry. Use your brain to avoid problems, and if you do encounter one, first use your brain to try to correct the situation. Only use your cell phone, if it works, in true emergencies. If it doesn't work down low in a valley, try hiking to a high point where you might get reception.

HIKING WITH CHILDREN

Hiking with children isn't a matter of how many miles you can cover or how much elevation gain you make in a day; it's about seeing and experiencing nature through their eyes.

Kids like to explore and have fun. They like to stop and point out bugs and plants, look under rocks, jump in puddles, and throw sticks. If you're taking a toddler or young child on a hike, start with a trail that you're familiar with. Trails that have interesting things for kids, like piles of leaves to play in or a small stream to wade through during the summer, will make the hike much more enjoyable for them and will keep them from getting bored.

You can keep your child's attention if you have a strategy before starting on the trail. Using games is not only an effective way to keep a child's attention, it's also a great way to teach him or her about nature. Quiz children on the names of plants and animals. Pick up a family-friendly outdoor hobby like Geocaching (www.geocaching .com) or Letterboxing (www.atlasquest.com), both of which combine the outdoors, clue solving, and treasure hunting. If your children are old enough, let them carry their own daypack filled with snacks and water. So that you are sure to go at their pace and not yours, let them lead the way. Playing follow the leader works particularly well when you have a group of children. Have each child take a turn at being the leader.

With children a lot of clothing is key. The only thing predictable about weather is that it will change. Especially in mountainous areas, weather can change dramatically in a very short time. Always bring extra clothing for children, regardless of the season. In the winter have your children wear wool socks and warm layers such as

long underwear, a fleece jacket and hat, wool mittens, and good rain gear. It's not a bad idea to have these along in late fall and early spring as well. Good footwear is also important. A sturdy pair of high-top tennis shoes or lightweight hiking boots is the best bet for little ones. If you're hiking in the summer near a lake or stream, bring along a pair of old sneakers that your child can put on when he wants to go exploring in the water. Remember that when you're near any type of water, always watch your child at all times. Also, keep a close eye on teething toddlers who may decide a rock or leaf of poison oak is an interesting item to put in their mouth.

From spring through fall you'll want your kids to wear a wide-brimmed hat to keep their face, head, and ears protected from the hot sun. Also, make sure your children wear sunscreen at all times. Choose a brand without PABA—children have sensitive skin and may have an allergic reaction to sunscreen that contains PABA. If you are hiking with a child younger than 6 months, don't use sunscreen or insect repellent. Instead, be sure that his or her head, face, neck, and ears are protected from the sun with a wide-brimmed hat and that all other skin exposed to the sun is protected with the appropriate clothing.

Remember that food is fun. Kids like snacks, so it's important to bring a lot of munchies for the trail. Stopping often for snack breaks is a fun way to keep the trail interesting. Raisins, apples, granola bars, crackers and cheese, cereal, and trail mix all make great snacks. Also, a few of their favorite candy treats can go a long way toward heading off a fit of fussing. If your child is old enough to carry her own backpack, let her fill it with some lightweight "comfort" items such as a doll, a small stuffed animal, or a little toy (you'll have to draw the line at bringing the 10-pound Tonka truck). If your kids don't like drinking water, you can bring some powdered drink mix or a juice box.

Avoid poorly designed child-carrying packs—you don't want to break your back carrying your child. Most child-carrying backpacks designed to hold a 40-pound child will contain a large carrying pocket to hold diapers and other items. Some have an optional rain/sun hood.

HIKING WITH YOUR DOG

Bringing your furry friend with you is always more fun than leaving him behind. Our canine pals make great trail buddies because they never complain and always make good company. Hiking with your dog can be a rewarding experience, especially if you plan ahead.

Getting your dog in shape. Before you plan outdoor adventures with your dog, make sure he's in shape for the trail. Getting your dog into shape takes the same discipline as getting yourself into shape, but luckily, your dog can get in shape with you. Take

◀ *A father-daughter moment at Delicate Arch*

your dog with you on your daily runs or walks. If there is a park near your house, hit a tennis ball or play Frisbee with your dog.

Swimming is also an excellent way to get your dog into shape. If there is a lake or river near where you live and your dog likes the water, have him retrieve a tennis ball or stick. Gradually build your dog's stamina up over a 2- to 3-month period. A good rule of thumb is to assume that your dog will travel twice as far as you will on the trail. If you plan on doing a 5-mile hike, be sure your dog is in shape for a 10-mile hike.

Training your dog for the trail. Before you go on your first hiking adventure with your dog, be sure he has a firm grasp on the basics of canine etiquette and behavior. Make sure he can sit, lie down, stay, and come. One of the most important commands you can teach your canine pal is to "come" under any situation. It's easy for your friend's nose to lead him astray or possibly get him lost. Another helpful command is the "get behind" command. When you're on a hiking trail that's narrow, you can have your dog follow behind you when other trail users approach. Nothing is more bothersome than an enthusiastic dog that runs back and forth on the trail and disrupts the peace of the trail for others—or, worse, jumps up on other hikers and gets them muddy. When you see other trail users approaching you on the trail, give them the right of way by quietly stepping off the trail and making your dog lie down and stay until they pass.

Equipment. The most critical pieces of equipment you can invest in for your dog are proper identification and a sturdy leash. Flexi-leads work well for hiking because they give your dog more freedom to explore but still leave you in control. Make sure your dog has identification that includes your name and address and a number for your veterinarian. Other forms of identification for your dog include a tattoo or a microchip. You should consult your veterinarian for more information on these last two options.

The next piece of equipment you'll want to consider is a pack for your dog. By no means should you hold all of your dog's essentials in your pack—let him carry his own gear! Dogs that are in good shape can carry 30 to 40 percent of their own weight.

Most packs are fitted by a dog's weight and girth measurement. Companies that make dog packs generally include guidelines to help you pick out the size that's right for your dog. Some characteristics to look for when purchasing a pack for your dog include a harness that contains two padded girth straps, a padded chest strap, leash attachments, removable saddlebags, internal water bladders, and external gear cords.

You can introduce your dog to the pack by first placing the empty pack on his back and letting him wear it around the yard. Keep an eye on him during this first introduction. He may decide to chew through the straps if you aren't watching him closely. Once he learns to treat the pack as an object of fun and not a foreign enemy,

◀ *Plan ahead for picking up after your dog.*

fill the pack evenly on both sides with a few ounces of dog food in resealable plastic bags. Have your dog wear his pack on your daily walks for a period of 2 to 3 weeks. Each week add a little more weight to the pack until your dog will accept carrying the maximum amount of weight he can carry.

You can also purchase collapsible water and dog food bowls for your dog. These bowls are lightweight and can easily be stashed into your pack or your dog's. If you are hiking on rocky terrain or in the snow, you can purchase footwear for your dog that will protect his feet from cuts and bruises.

Always carry plastic bags to remove feces from the trail. It is a courtesy to other trail users and helps protect local wildlife.

The following is a list of items to bring when you take your dog hiking: collapsible water bowls, a comb, a collar and a leash, dog food, plastic bags for feces, a dog pack, flea/tick powder, paw protection, water, and a first-aid kit that contains eye ointment, tweezers, scissors, stretchy foot wrap, gauze, antibacterial wash, sterile cotton tip applicators, antibiotic ointment, and cotton wrap. Your dog is just as prone—if not more prone—to getting in trouble on the trail as you are, so be prepared. Here's a rundown of the more likely misfortunes that might befall your little friend.

Bees and wasps. If a bee or wasp stings your dog, remove the stinger with a pair of tweezers and place a mudpack or a cloth dipped in cold water over the affected area.

Porcupines. One good reason to keep your dog on a leash is to prevent it from getting a nose full of porcupine quills. You may be able to remove the quills with pliers, but a veterinarian is the best person to do this nasty job because most dogs need to be sedated.

Heat stroke. Avoid hiking with your dog in really hot weather. Dogs with heat stroke will pant excessively, lie down and refuse to get up, and become lethargic and disoriented. If your dog shows any of these signs on the trail, have him lie down in the shade. If you are near a stream, pour cool water over your dog's entire body to help bring his body temperature back to normal.

Heartworm. Dogs get heartworms from mosquitoes, which carry the disease in the prime mosquito months of July and August. Giving your dog a monthly pill prescribed by your veterinarian easily prevents this condition.

Plant pitfalls. If you have a long-haired dog, consider trimming the hair between his toes and giving him a summer haircut to help prevent plants from becoming tangled in your dog's fur. After every hike always look over your dog for burs and other seeds—especially between his toes and his ears.

Rock outcropping overlooking the San Juan River (hike 25)

Other plant hazards include burs, thorns, thistles, and poison ivy. If you find any burs or thistles on your dog, remove them as soon as possible before they become an unmanageable mat. Thorns can pierce a dog's foot and cause a great deal of pain. If you see that your dog is lame, stop and check his feet for thorns. Dogs are not immune to poison ivy, and they can pick up the sticky, oily substance from the plant and transfer it to you.

Protect those paws. Be sure to keep your dog's nails trimmed so he avoids getting soft tissue or joint injuries. If your dog slows and refuses to go on, check to see that his paws aren't torn or worn. You can protect your dog's paws from trail hazards such as sharp gravel and thorns by purchasing dog boots. Ruff Wear makes an excellent pair that is both sturdy and stays on dogs' feet.

Sunburn. If your dog has light skin, he is an easy target for sunburn on his nose and other exposed skin areas. You can apply a nontoxic sunscreen to exposed skin areas that will help protect him from overexposure to the sun.

Mushrooms spring up after a late summer rain near Wilson Peak.

Ticks and fleas. Ticks can easily give your dog Lyme disease, as well as other diseases. Before you hit the trail, treat your dog with a flea and tick spray or powder. You can also ask your veterinarian about a once-a-month pour-on treatment that repels fleas and ticks.

Mosquitoes and deer flies. These little flying machines can do a job on your dog's snout and ears. Best bet is to spray your dog with fly repellent for horses to discourage both pests.

Giardia. Dogs can get Giardia, which results in diarrhea. It is usually not debilitating, but it's definitely messy. A vaccine against Giardia is available.

Mushrooms. Make sure your dog doesn't sample mushrooms along the trail. They could be poisonous to him, but he doesn't know that.

When you are finally ready to hit the trail with your dog, keep in mind that national parks and many wilderness areas do not allow dogs on trails. Your best bet is to hike in national forests, BLM lands, and state parks. Always call ahead to see what the restrictions are.

Hike Index

American Hiking Society

Because you

hike.

We're with you
every step of the way

As a national voice for hikers, **American Hiking Society** works every day:

- Building and maintaining hiking trails
- Educating and supporting hikers by providing information and resources
- Supporting hiking and trail organizations nationwide
- Speaking for hikers in the halls of Congress and with federal land managers

Whether you're a casual hiker or a seasoned backpacker, become a member of American Hiking Society and join the national hiking community! You'll enjoy great member benefits and help preserve the nation's hiking trails, so tomorrow's hike is even better than today's. We invite you to join us now!

American Hiking Society

32953012582997

ABOUT THE AUTHORS

JD Tanner grew up playing and exploring in the hills of southern Illinois. He has earned a degree in Outdoor Recreation from Southeast Missouri State University and an advanced degree in Outdoor Recreation from Southern Illinois University in Carbondale. He has traveled extensively throughout the United States and is the Director of Recreation at San Juan College.

Emily Ressler-Tanner grew up splitting time between southeastern Missouri and southeastern Idaho. She spent her early years fishing, hiking, and camping with her family. In college she enjoyed trying out many new outdoor activities and eventually graduated from Southern Illinois University in Carbondale with an advanced degree in Recreation Resource Administration.

Together they have climbed, paddled, hiked, and camped all over the United States. They co-instructed college-level, outdoor recreation courses for several years before joining the staff at the Leave No Trace Center for Outdoor Ethics as Traveling Trainers. Former residents of Farmington, New Mexico, JD and Emily now reside in southern Illinois.

FalconGuides they have written or revised include:

Best Easy Day Hikes Grand Staircase-Escalante — Revised
Best Easy Day Hikes Missouri Ozarks
Best Easy Day Hikes Springfield, Missouri
Best Hikes Near St. Louis
Best Hikes Near Albuquerque
Hiking Grand Staircase-Escalante — Revised
Best Easy Day Hikes St. Louis
Hiking Ozarks